Give Me Five!

PUPIL'S BOOK 4

macmillan education

Joanne Ramsden • Donna Shaw

Contents

What does (your brother) look like?
He's got (short, blonde) hair and (brown) eyes.
Has (he) got (a beard)? Yes, he has. No, he hasn't.

We must (speak English in class).
We're going to (work together).

Literacy	Culture	21st Century Skills	Cross-curricular links
Text type: A recipe	Street food in New York City	**Ways of working:** collaboration and teamwork	**Science:** Food and nutrition; Classifying food; Nutrients; A healthy, balanced diet **Arts and Crafts:** Observing patterns; Still life
Text type: A biography / an autobiography	Famous Hawaiian people	**Ways of working:** researching information and planning a presentation	**Science:** Our body; Stages of life; Growing up **Arts and Crafts:** Expressive portraits
Text type: An encyclopaedia entry	Dinosaur fossils in Canada	**Digital skills:** exploring virtual museums	**Science:** Animal groups **Arts and Crafts:** Complementing colours; Symbols
Designing a minibeast exhibition		**Science:** Plants; How insects help with pollination	
Text type: A fact file	An observatory in Australia	**Ways of thinking:** grading things / putting things on a cline	**Science:** Our planet; Celestial bodies; The solar system **Arts and Crafts:** Skyscapes; Swirls, spirals, curved and wavy lines, continuous lines
Text type: A myth / a mythical creature	A music festival in New Zealand	**Living in the world:** making your own fun	**Science:** Forms of energy; Sound **Arts and Crafts:** Reflection, horizontal and vertical symmetry
Text type: An advert	Robot competitions in the USA	**Digital skills:** creating adverts	**Science:** Machines; Machines that use electricity; How a complex machine works **Arts and Crafts:** Geometric and organic forms
Creating an action plan to make your school green		**Science:** Matter; The three Rs – Reduce, Reuse and Recycle	
Text type: An acrostic poem	Transport in Hong Kong	**Ways of thinking:** making predictions based on existing knowledge	**Science:** Living together; The area where we live **Arts and Crafts:** Perspective lines and depth
Text type: A newspaper article / an interview	Lighthouse keepers in Tasmania	**Living in the world:** health and safety	**Science:** Population; The active population **Arts and Crafts:** Depth, overlap and size
Text type: A travel brochure	What's England famous for?	**Digital skills:** getting information from different sources	**Science:** Population; The population of different countries **Arts and Crafts:** Positive and negative space
Planning a medieval festival day		**Science:** History; The Middle Ages	

Cambridge Exams Practice Practice for the CYLE A1 Movers exam and A2 Flyers exam (see p.127 for syllabus)

Unit Starter Welcome back, Luke!

1 Find and say.

- five sea animals
- five water sports
- five pieces of water sports equipment
- five free-time activities
- five numbers
- five foods
- five places in a town

2 Listen and read. Act out. CD1 01

3 Listen and sing *This is my best friend*. CD1 02

4 Talk Partners Ask and answer about someone in your family.

What's his / her name? How old is he / she?
What does he / she do? What does he / she like doing?

Key learning outcomes: review level 3 vocabulary; ask for and give information about other people **Language:** *His name's Luke. He's (23). What does he do? He's a scientist.*

♫
This is my best friend.
Her name's Lily.
She's nine years old.
She likes taking photos
And singing songs.
She's my best friend.

This is my best friend.
His name's Josh.
He's ten years old.
He likes swimming
And sailing boats.
He's my best friend.

This is our best friend.
His name's Ravi.
He's ten years old.
He likes doing puzzles
And making things.
He's our best friend. ♫

1 Listen and read. Act out. CD1 04

What does your brother look like?

He's got short, blonde hair and brown eyes.

Has he got a beard or a moustache?

No, he hasn't.

Has he got freckles?

No, he hasn't.

2 Listen and repeat. CD1 05

blonde hair	moustache	ponytail	curly hair
freckles	beard	straight hair	wavy hair

3 Talk Partners Ask and answer about a friend.

What does your friend look like?

She's got short, wavy hair and freckles.

Key learning outcomes: use adjectives to describe physical appearance
Language: *What does he look like? He's got short blonde hair and brown eyes.*

1 **Listen and read. Act out.** CD1 06

Welcome home, Luke!

Key learning outcomes: read, listen and understand a story about Lily, Ravi, Josh and Luke
Language: *He's got a beard. I love going snorkelling.*

1 Talk Partners Ask and answer.

A	B	C	D	E	F	G	H	I	J	K	L	M
153	177	195	231	245	269	311	333	389	421	457	495	501
N	**O**	**P**	**Q**	**R**	**S**	**T**	**U**	**V**	**W**	**X**	**Y**	**Z**
585	637	645	671	715	759	783	849	853	871	923	947	999

2 Cooperative learning Read and listen. CD1 08

Our class contract

Our class rules

1 We must speak English in class.

2 We must put our hands up to speak.

3 We must take turns and listen to each other.

Our class promises

1 We're going to work together.

2 We're going to share our things.

Key learning outcomes: identify and say letters and numbers 100–1000; use *must* and *going to* to talk about obligations and responsibilities in the classroom **Language:** *We must speak English in class.*

Let's eat!

1 flour

2 oil

3 nuts

4 biscuits

5 chocolate chips

6 sugar

7 salt

8 raisins

9 jam

10 butter

11 coconut

12 cream

1 What's your favourite type of cake? What ingredients do you need to make a cake? Make a list. Brainstorm ???

2 Listen, point and say the vocabulary chant. CD1 10

3 Listen, look and sing *Let's go shopping!* CD1 11

Let's go shopping! Make a list.
Look in the cupboard
And in the fridge.

Is there any flour in the cupboard?
Is there any butter in the fridge?
Are there any nuts?
Are there any chocolate chips?
Is there any sugar?
Let me see!
Chorus

Is there any oil in the cupboard?
Is there any cream in the fridge?
Are there any biscuits?
Are there any raisins?
Is there any coconut?
I don't know!
Chorus

4 **Talk Partners** **Look at the picture. Play a memory game.**

Is there any sugar in the cupboard?

Yes, there is.

Are there any nuts in the fridge?

No, there aren't.

Key learning outcomes: identify and say ingredients; sing a song about going shopping
Vocabulary: ingredients for making a cake

1 **Listen and read. Listen and repeat. Act out.** CD1 13

Luke: Let's make a cake for the festival. I've got a recipe for a Burfi cake from India.

Lily: Cool! Can I help?

Luke: Yes, please. We need some sugar.

Lily: How much sugar do we need?

Luke: We need a lot of sugar. We need some nuts, too.

Lily: How many nuts do we need?

Luke: We need a few nuts. We need some milk and some coconut, too.

Lily: OK. It's going to be delicious!

2 **Read again. Which ingredients do Luke and Lily need?**

3 **Talk Partners** **Listen and follow. Repeat.** CD1 14

Quantifiers

I You We They	need	a lot of some a few	nuts. biscuits. raisins.
He She	needs	a lot of some a little	butter. cream. flour.

Grammar clue

We use **How many** to ask questions about things we can count. How many nuts do they need?

We use **How much** to ask questions about things we can't count. How much sugar does he need?

4 **Talk Partners** **Ask and answer about the ingredients for the Burfi cake.**

Key learning outcomes: ask questions using *How much* and *How many;* identify and use countable and uncountable nouns **Grammar:** *How many nuts do they need? They need a few nuts.*

Before you read

1 Can you remember the ingredients for the Burfi cake?

2 Listen and read. Act out. CD1 15

Read the title of the story. What do you think goes wrong with the Burfi cake?

The Burfi cake disaster

Key learning outcomes: read, listen and understand a story about a Burfi cake

Language: *What do we need to do now? Add the sugar and stir.*

After you read

3 **Talk Partners** **Ask and answer.**

1 Who chops the nuts?

> Josh chops the nuts.

2 Do they add a lot of milk?

3 How much sugar do they need?

4 What does Ravi give to Josh?

5 What does Luke's friend bring?

4 **Values** **Read and discuss.** Whole Class

- Who isn't paying attention in the story? Why?
- What happens because Ravi isn't paying attention?
- Do you pay attention when people talk to you?
- What happens when you don't pay attention?

5 **Use the code to read the message from Luke.**

> I'm going travelling again. Can you guess where I'm going? I'm going to 585-245-871 947-637-715-457 195-389-783-947. See you!

1 Listen, point and say. CD1 17

1 stir

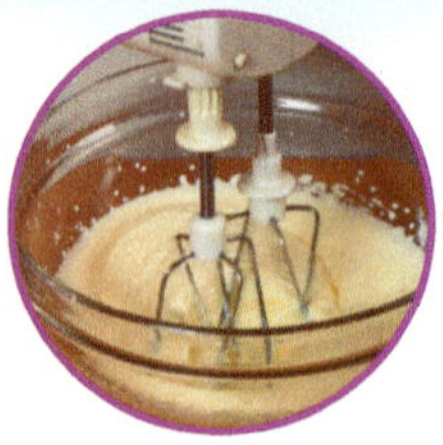

2 mix

3 chop

4 heat

5 pour

6 add

2 Listen and sing *Let's make soup!* CD1 18

Let's make soup!
Let's make soup!
What do we need to do
To make delicious soup?

First, we need to get a pan.
Next, we chop the carrots.
Mix some green beans,
Onions and tomatoes.
Then, we put them in the pan.

Chorus

After that, we need to add the water.
Then, we heat it up.
Finally, cook the ingredients all together.
Stir it all the time.

Chorus

3 Listen and follow. Repeat. CD1 19

need to

		I			
		you			add?
What	do	we	need	to	do?
		they			chop?
	does	he			stir?
		she			

4 Talk Partners Ask and answer.

What do we need to chop?

We need to chop the carrots.

Grammar clue

We use **do** with *I*, *you*, *we* and *they*.
We use **does** with *he* and *she*.

Key learning outcomes: identify and say verbs for cooking; use *need to* to talk about requirements **Vocabulary:** cooking verbs **Grammar:** *We need to (chop) the carrots.*

1 Listen, read and say. CD1 20

Speak and spell

'i_e' or 'ie'?

Remember!

light fly

Spike likes rice and Mike likes pies and wearing a tie.

Now practise spelling on page 10 in your Activity Book.

2 Read the recipe. Listen and identify five differences. CD1 21

Listening tip!
Read the recipe carefully before you listen.

Banana bread

You need:

some flour	a lot of butter
2 eggs	a little salt
some sugar	a few bananas
a lot of milk	

Mix the sugar and the butter.
Add the eggs and pour the milk into the bowl.
Cut the bananas and stir in the flour.
Heat the oven and cook for 40 minutes.

3 **Talk Partners** Ask and answer to complete the recipe.

Teacher's Resource Bank: Unit 1

Key learning outcomes: listen for specific information; play a communication game using *How much / How many* and *need to* **Phonics:** Alternative vowel spellings: *i_e – ie*

Before you read

1. Look at the photo on the recipe. What ingredients do you think you need to make a Knickerbocker glory? Make a list. *Whole Class*

2. Read the text quickly. Do you think a Knickerbocker glory is healthy? *Whole Class*

3. Read and listen. What's the last ingredient you add to a Knickerbocker glory? What's your favourite ingredient? CD1 22

Knickerbocker glory

Ingredients

- biscuits
- vanilla and chocolate ice cream
- raspberry sauce
- chocolate chips
- chopped nuts
- cream
- cherries

Equipment

a bowl

a spoon

an ice cream scoop

an ice cream dish

Preparation time: 10 minutes

Instructions

1. First, break the biscuits into pieces. Put the biscuit pieces in the dish.
2. Next, add two scoops of chocolate ice cream and one scoop of vanilla ice cream to the dish.
3. Then, pour a little raspberry sauce on the ice cream.
4. After that, mix a few chocolate chips with the chopped nuts in a bowl.
5. Next, sprinkle the nuts and chocolate chips on the ice cream.
6. Then, add the cream.
7. Finally, add the cherries on top.

Serving instructions

Serve straight away.

After you read

Go to page 11 in your Activity Book.

Key learning outcomes: read and understand an instructional text

Text type: **a recipe**

Investigate a text

1 What ingredients do you think you need to make these pizzas? Which pizza do you prefer? *(Whole Class)*

1

2

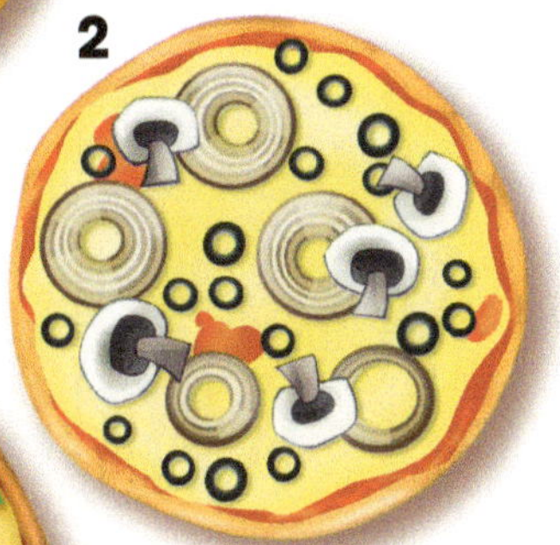

3

2 Read and listen. Which picture in Activity 1 is the pizza for this recipe? CD1 23

Reading tip!
Use the photo to help you identify all the ingredients in the pizza.

Tuna and vegetable pizza

Ingredients
- mushrooms
- onions
- peppers
- oil
- sweetcorn
- tomato sauce
- cheese
- a pizza base
- tuna
- olives

Equipment

a chopping board

a pan

a knife

a spoon

Preparation time	Cooking time
10 minutes	15 minutes

Instructions

1. First, chop the mushrooms, onions and peppers.
2. Next, heat the oil in a pan.
3. Then, add the chopped vegetables to the pan and cook for one minute. Stir it all the time. Add the sweetcorn.
4. After that, add the tomato sauce and cheese to the pizza base. Then, add the tuna.
5. Next, add the vegetables. Put the olives on top of the pizza.
6. Finally, cook the pizza in the oven for 15 minutes.

Discuss a text

3 Think and discuss. *(Whole Class)*

1. Look at the layout of the recipe. Where's the list of ingredients and equipment?
2. Are the instructions in order? Are they numbered?
3. Is there a photo of the end result?
4. Where can you see how long it takes to make the pizza?

Writing tip!
We use ***First*** to start the recipe instructions.
We use ***Next***, ***Then*** and ***After that*** for the following instructions.
We use ***Finally*** for the last instruction.

→ **Plan and write a recipe on page 12 in your Activity Book.**

1 **Read Luke's questions. What do you think?** Whole Class

I'm in **New York City** now. It's the city that never sleeps! You can find every type of food at any time of the day. Can you answer these questions?

1 Which food can you eat in a hard shell?
2 Which food is big and salty?
3 Which food can you eat with salad or vegetables?
4 Which food is from Belgium?

2 **Read and listen. Answer Luke's questions.** CD1 24

street food in New York City

Street food in New York City

Tacos in New York City are delicious. The best place to eat them is from a cart on a street corner. Tacos in New York City are served in a hard shell. Try them with beef or chicken and refried beans. You can add chopped onions, peppers and grated cheese.

Squeeze a lime over your taco to complete the taco experience!

New York City is great because you can find food from all over the world. You can buy waffles from Belgium. They're delicious with cream, melted chocolate and strawberries.

There are pretzel stands in New York City, too. The pretzels are very big, warm and salty. They're delicious!

For a different type of savoury snack, you can try falafel. It's made from chickpeas, and people eat it on thin bread. For a healthy option, try it with lots of salad or vegetables.

Some diners stay open ALL NIGHT!

Think about your culture **What types of street food can you eat in your country? Do you like street food? Can you find food from other countries where you live?**

Do the New York City web quest and the Unit Review on pages 13 and 14 in your Activity Book. ICT

Key learning outcomes: read about street food in New York City; think about and research New York City

21 CHANNEL

Welcome back to Channel 21! Our first programme this year is about street food. What street food do you like?

1 **Watch the video. Which street food isn't in the video?**

2 **Watch the video again. Read and say *true* or *false*. Correct the false sentences.**

1 A falafel sandwich can't be healthy.

2 Pretzels are cold and sweet.

3 All the stalls serve savoury food.

4 There's only one type of sundae.

5 You can't eat pancakes for breakfast.

3 **Work in a group. Choose two ingredients to add to each food and explain why.**

Teamwork

When you work in a team, you need to take turns, speak clearly and listen to each other.

1 **Waffle:** strawberries, chocolate, cream

2 **Falafel sandwich:** onions, tomatoes, lettuce

3 **Ice cream sundae:** nuts, cherries, bananas

4 **Pancakes:** butter, syrup, sugar

Key learning outcomes: watch and understand a video about street food
21st **Ways of working:** collaboration and teamwork

Unit 2 What are you like?

1 tidy

2 untidy

3 confident

4 shy

5 active

6 lazy

7 friendly

8 unfriendly

9 quiet

10 noisy

11 kind

12 unkind

1 **Think of different family members. What are they like? Make a list of words to describe them.** Brainstorm

2 **Listen, point and say the vocabulary chant.** CD1 28

3 **Listen, look and sing** ***What's she like?*** CD1 29

This is my aunt.
What's she like?
Is she kind, confident or shy?
She's out and about.
She's always helping people.
She's very kind.

This is my uncle.
What's he like?
Is he tidy, active or lazy?
He's out and about.
He's always doing exercise.
He's very active.

This is my grandma.
What's she like?
Is she friendly, quiet or noisy?
She's out and about.
She's always making friends.
She's very friendly.

4 **Talk Partners** **Ask and answer.**

Are you lazy?

No, I'm not. I'm active.

What's your grandma like?

She's confident and kind.

Key learning outcomes: identify and say adjectives of character; sing a song about what people are like **Vocabulary:** adjectives of character

1 Listen and read. Listen and repeat. Act out. CD1 31

Josh: Hi, Grandma. Can you help me with my school project, please?

Grandma: Yes, of course.

Josh: What were you like when you were young? Were you tidy?

Grandma: No, I wasn't. When I was young, I was very untidy.

Josh: Were you confident?

Grandma: No, I wasn't. I was very shy.

Josh: Were you active?

Grandma: Yes, I was. I'm active now, too. It's time for my yoga class. I don't want to be late.

Josh: Thank you, Grandma. Have fun!

2 Read again. What was grandma like when she was young?

3 Listen and follow. Repeat. CD1 32

Past simple: *be*

I He She	was wasn't	active. lazy. tidy.
You We They	were weren't	untidy. shy. confident.

4 Talk Partners Play a *true* or *false* game.

I was tidy when I was young.

I think it's false.

Yes, it's false.

Grammar clue

Were you untidy? Yes, I **was**.

Was she quiet? Yes, she **was**.

Key learning outcomes: use the past simple of *be* and adjectives of character to talk about what people were like when they were young **Grammar:** *She wasn't tidy. I was confident when I was young.*

Before you read

1 **Use the code to read the message from Luke.**

Yesterday, I was at the 871-153-923 501-849-759-245-849-501. It was great!

Read the title of the story. Who do you think plays the trick? What do you think happens?

2 **Listen and read. Act out.** CD1 33

The trick that went wrong

Key learning outcomes: read, listen and understand a story about a trick that went wrong

Language: *I visited the wax museum when I was seven.*

After you read

3 Talk Partners **Ask and answer.**

1 Where do Josh, Lily and Ravi go?

They go to the wax museum.

2 Do they see a waxwork of a sportsperson?

3 What was Christopher Columbus like?

4 Who plays a trick?

5 How does the trick go wrong?

4 Values **Read and discuss.** Whole Class

- Is Lily sorry when she plays a trick on Ravi and Josh?
- Do you play tricks on your friends?
- How do your friends feel when you play tricks on them?
- How do you feel when your friends play tricks on you?

1 Listen, point and say. CD1 35

1 learn to walk

2 start nursery school

3 move house

4 get a pet

5 go on a plane

6 write a story

2 Listen and sing *I was a very special person*. CD1 36

I was a very special person
From the minute I was born.

I learnt to walk and talk when I was one.
I started nursery school when I was three.
My teacher said I was fantastic
And now just look at me!

Chorus

I moved house when I was five.
I wrote a story when I was eight.
My teacher said I was fantastic
And now she says I'm great!

Chorus

3 Listen and follow. Repeat. CD1 37

Past simple: regular and irregular verbs

I	learnt to walk		I		ten months old.
He	started nursery school		he		one.
She	moved house	when	she	was	three.
You	got a pet		you	were	five.
We	went on a plane		we		seven.
They	wrote a story		they		eight.

4 Talk Partners

Make true sentences.

I started school when I was five.

I got a pet when I was seven.

Grammar clue

We use *Did* to ask questions about the past.

Did you learn to walk when you were one?

Yes, I **did**. No, I **didn't**.

Key learning outcomes: identify and say past activities; use past simple verbs to ask and answer about past activities **Vocabulary:** past activities **Grammar:** *I started school when I was five.*

1 Listen, read and say. CD1 38

Speak and spell

'y' or 'ey'?

A very noisy monkey and a very lazy donkey drop the key for the lorry down the chimney.

Remember!

meat tree

Now practise spelling on page 20 in your Activity Book.

2 Read the questionnaire. Listen and identify five differences. CD1 39

When did you do these things?

Name: Alice Brown Age: 10

Activity	Age	Activity	Age
1 Write a story	six	4 Start nursery school	three
2 Go on a plane	five	5 Move house	five
3 Learn to walk	ten months old	6 Get a first pet	eight

3 Talk Partners Ask and answer to complete the questionnaire. Find three similarities.

Speaking tip!

Take turns to ask and answer the questions.

Teacher's Resource Bank: Unit 2

Key learning outcomes: listen for specific information; play a communication game using the past simple **Phonics:** Alternative vowel spellings: *y – ie*

Before you read

1 What's the difference between a biography and an autobiography? Whole Class

2 You are going to read a biography about Roald Dahl. Do you know any of his books? Which one is your favourite? Whole Class

3 Read and listen. CD1 40

Roald Dahl

Home | Biography | Publications

Roald Dahl

Roald Dahl was born in Wales in 1916. When he was a boy, he loved reading books and listening to stories. His mother told him stories about trolls and other mythical creatures.

Roald Dahl started writing a secret diary when he was eight. He wrote in the diary every day and he hid it in an enormous conker tree in the garden.

Roald Dahl started boarding school when he was nine. He didn't like it. He was excellent at sports, but he wasn't very good at writing stories!

When he was 13, he started a new school. The school was near a chocolate factory. Roald loved chocolate, but he didn't like chocolate cake or chocolate ice cream.

He wrote his first children's book in 1943. It was called *The Gremlins*. Then, he started writing more books for adults. He didn't write another story for children until 1961, when he wrote *James and the Giant Peach*. He wrote *Charlie and the Chocolate Factory* after that. Roald Dahl wrote over 20 books for children. He always wrote his stories in pencil on yellow paper. Roald Dahl's stories were very popular, but he only won a few prizes, including one for *The Witches* in 1983 and another for *Matilda* in 1988. His books are still very popular today. There are films of some of his books, too.

He once said, 'If you're going to get anywhere in life, you have to read a lot of books.'

After you read

Go to page 21 in your Activity Book.

Key learning outcomes: read and understand a chronological account

Text type: **A biography / an autobiography**

Investigate a text

1 **In what order do you think this information appears in Ben's autobiography?** Whole Class

I started nursery school. I moved house. I was born. I started primary school. I learnt to read and write. I got a pet. I learnt to walk. I learnt to talk.

2 **Read and listen to find out.** CD1 41

My name's Ben. I was born in London in 2009. I lived with my mum, my dad, my two sisters and my brother in a small flat in the centre of London.

I learnt to walk when I was one. I learnt to talk when I was one and a half. My first words were 'mum' and 'bye'.

I started nursery school when I was three. I started primary school when I was five. In my first year, I learnt to read and write. I was a bit shy and untidy when I was young. I was very active and I loved playing basketball at the weekend.

We moved house when I was eight. My new house has got a big garden, so I got my first pet – a cat called Joey. He's very friendly!

Discuss a text

3 **Think and discuss.** Whole Class

1 What information is at the start of the autobiography?

2 Are the events in chronological order?

3 Does the writer use *I*, *he*, *she*, *we*, *you* or *they*?

4 Is the information in the present, the past simple or both?

Writing tip!

When you include speech in your text, remember to use **inverted commas.**

My first words were 'mum' and 'bye'.

→ **Plan and write your autobiography on page 22 in your Activity Book.**

Key learning outcomes: prepare and write your autobiography; use inverted commas

1 Read Luke's questions. What do you think?

Whole Class

1 Which President of the USA was born in Hawaii?
2 Who was the first king of Hawaii?
3 What was Ellison Onizuka's job?
4 What's Bruno Mars' real name?

2 Read and listen. Answer Luke's questions.

CD1 42

Hawaiian people

Hawaiian people

ELLISON ONIZUKA was born in Hawaii in 1946. He was the first NASA astronaut from Hawaii. He first went into space in 1985. He was very active and enjoyed running, fishing and outdoor sports. The Onizuka Centre for International Astronomy in Hawaii is named after him. You can use the telescopes at the centre to look at the stars.

BARACK OBAMA was born in Hawaii in 1961. He became the 44th President of the USA on 20th January 2009. His father was from Kenya and his mother was from Kansas in the USA. He lived with his grandparents when he was young. Barack Obama studied Law at university. He's very active and hard-working.

KAMEHAMEHA THE GREAT was the first king of Hawaii. Tradition says that he was born on a stormy night when a bright star appeared in the sky. He stopped the Hawaiian people fighting. In Hawaii, people celebrate King Kamehameha Day on 11th June. There's a parade with marching bands, horses and lots of flowers.

BRUNO MARS was born in Hawaii in 1985. His real name is Peter Gene Hernandez. He was confident and independent when he was young and he loved music. Bruno writes songs, sings and plays the guitar, the piano and the drums. He has won lots of prizes for his music.

In Hawaii, 'Aloha' means 'Hello'!

Think about your culture Can you name some famous people from your country? What are they famous for? Who's your favourite famous person?

Do the Hawaii web quest and the Unit Review on pages 23 and 24 in your Activity Book. ICT

Key learning outcomes: read about famous Hawaiian people; think about and research Hawaii

21 CHANNEL

1 **Watch the video. Why are these people heroes?**

2 **Watch the video again. Read and answer the questions.**

1 Can firefighters get ready quickly?
2 When did Andy Murray start playing tennis?
3 When was Emma Watson born?
4 Are doctors kind and confident?
5 When did Adele write her first song?

3 **Choose a hero. Find out information to plan a presentation about your hero.** ICT

Planning a presentation

1 What's special about your hero?
2 How old is your hero?
3 What's your hero like?
4 What was your hero like when he / she was young?
5 Why is he / she your hero?

Key learning outcomes: watch and understand a video about heroes
21st **Ways of working:** researching information and planning a presentation

Unit 3

A long time ago

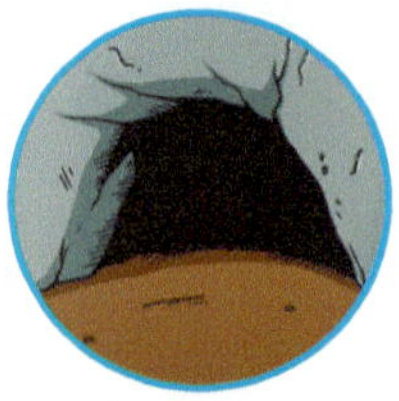

1 cave

2 basket

3 axe

4 spear

5 knife

6 bones

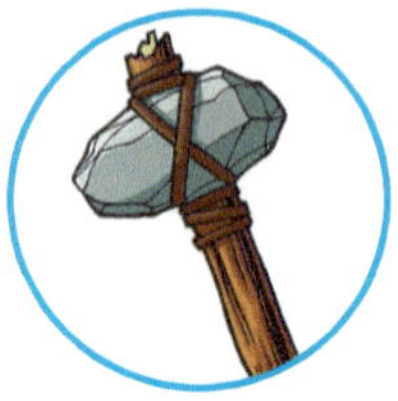

7 hammer

8 fire

9 bowl

10 tools

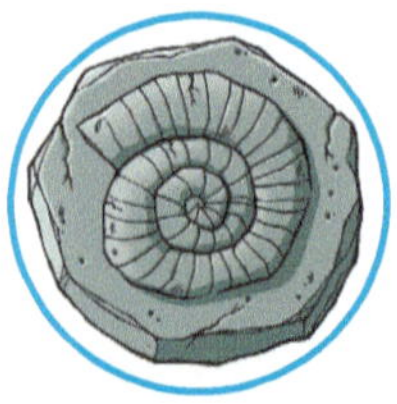

11 fossil

12 fur

1 Are there any museums where you live? What can you see in museums? Make a list. Brainstorm

2 Listen, point and say the vocabulary chant. CD1 46

3 Listen, look and sing *In prehistoric times*. CD1 47

A long time ago
In prehistoric times,
Cave men and women
Walked the Earth.

They wore fur.
They ate meat and fish.
They made fire
With stones on the ground.
Chorus

They had axes.
They had spears.
They had tools
To help them hunt and fish.
Chorus

4 Talk Partners **Ask and answer.**

Were there tools in prehistoric times?

Yes, there were.

Were there computers in prehistoric times?

No, there weren't.

Key learning outcomes: identify and say prehistoric times vocabulary; sing a song about prehistoric times **Vocabulary:** prehistoric times

1 **Listen and read. Listen and repeat. Act out.** CD1 49

Lily: Yesterday, we went to the Natural History Museum.

Ravi: Wow! Did you learn a lot?

Lily: Yes, we did. We learnt about prehistoric times.

Ravi: Cool! Where did people live in prehistoric times?

Lily: They lived in caves.

Ravi: What did they wear?

Lily: They wore fur. They didn't have clothes like ours.

Ravi: Really? What did they eat?

Lily: They ate meat and fish.

Ravi: How did they cook their food?

Lily: They made fire with a special stone called flint.

2 **Read again. What did Lily see in the Natural History Museum?**

3 **Listen and follow. Repeat.** CD1 50

Past simple: questions

		I	eat?
What		you	wear?
When		he	hunt?
Where	did	she	live?
How		we	cook?
		they	make?

4 **Talk Partners**

Ask and answer about prehistoric times.

What did they cook?

They cooked meat and fish.

Grammar clue

What **did** prehistoric people **wear**? They **wore** fur.
What **did** prehistoric people **eat**? They **ate** fish.
Where **did** prehistoric people **live**? They **lived** in caves.

Key learning outcomes: use the past simple to ask and answer questions
Grammar: *What did they eat? They ate meat and fish.*

Before you read

1 **Use the code to read the message from Luke.**

Yesterday, I went 457–153–947–153–457–389–585–311 with my friends. We had a great time!

Read the title of the story. What do you think the children discover?

2 **Listen and read. Act out.** CD2 01

The important discovery

Key learning outcomes: read, listen and understand a story about an important discovery
Language: *It's behind those rocks. We found them in a cave.*

After you read

3 **Talk Partners** **Ask and answer.**

1 What did the children do today?

They went kayaking.

2 What did they wear?

3 What did Lily drop?

4 Where did they find it?

5 What did they find in the cave?

4 **Values** **Read and discuss.** Whole Class

- Why do you think the children followed the bottle?
- How do you feel when you see litter in the countryside?
- Why do you think it's important to put your litter in the bin?
- How can we make sure that people don't drop litter?

1 Listen, point and say. CD2 03

1 sabre-toothed tiger

2 giant ground sloth

3 prehistoric armadillo

4 dodo

5 sabre-toothed squirrel

6 woolly mammoth

2 Listen and sing *A long, long time ago*. CD2 04

There was a sabre-toothed tiger,
An armadillo, a squirrel and a sloth.
There were different animals
Many years ago.
Some of them are now extinct.

A dodo was a very strange bird.
It lived hundreds of years ago.
It could run, but it couldn't fly,
A long, long time ago.
Chorus

A woolly mammoth had
enormous tusks.
It lived thousands of years ago.
It could walk, but it couldn't jump,
A long, long time ago.
Chorus

An armadillo had a very hard shell.
It lived thousands of years ago.
It could swim, but it couldn't
climb trees,
A long, long time ago.
Chorus

3 Listen and follow. Repeat. CD2 05

could and couldn't

I		**walk.**
You		**fly.**
He/She		**swim.**
It	**could**	**jump.**
We	**couldn't**	**run.**
They		**climb.**

4 Talk Partners

Play a *true* or *false* game.

A dodo could fly.

That's false.

Grammar clue

We use *could* to talk about ability in the past.
Sabre-toothed squirrels **couldn't fly**.

Key learning outcomes: identify and say animals from the past; use *could* to talk about ability in the past **Vocabulary:** animals from the past **Grammar:** *It could jump.*

1 **Listen, read and say.** CD2 06

Speak and spell

Pau**l the parrot can dr**aw** with his cl**aw**s. S**au**l the squirrel drinks s**au**ce with his p**aw**s.**

➔ **Now practise spelling on page 30 in your Activity Book.**

2 **Read the prehistoric animal fact cards. Listen and identify five differences.** CD2 07

Listening tip!
Think about what you already know about the animals before you listen.

Name: Sabre-toothed tiger
Colour: Brown, yellow, black and white
Characteristics: They had fur and long, sharp teeth.
Abilities: They could run fast and climb trees. They could swim.
Food: They ate meat.

Name: Woolly mammoth
Colour: Light brown
Characteristics: They had long tusks and fur.
Abilities: They could walk and run. They couldn't jump and they couldn't climb trees.
Food: They ate grass, other plants and flowers.

Name: Dodo
Colour: Grey
Characteristics: They had a large beak.
Abilities: They could run. They couldn't swim and they couldn't fly.
Food: They ate fruit, seeds and nuts.

3 ➔ **Talk Partners** **Ask and answer to complete the chart.**

Teacher's Resource Bank: Unit 3

Key learning outcomes: listen for specific information; play a communication game using *could* **Phonics:** Alternative vowel spellings: *aw – au*

Before you read

1 You are going to read an encyclopaedia entry about dinosaurs. What do you want to know? Make a list of questions. Use these words.

Whole Class

What ...? When ...? Where ...? How ...?

2 Read and listen. Does the encyclopaedia entry answer your questions?

CD2 08

Dinosaurs

Dinosaurs were reptiles that dominated the Earth in prehistoric times. The first dinosaurs lived around 225 million years ago. We know about dinosaurs because archaeologists discovered dinosaur fossils buried in the ground. There were many different types of dinosaurs. Some dinosaurs were carnivores (they ate meat) and others were herbivores (they ate plants). Some dinosaurs could run very fast and others were very slow.

Tyrannosaurus

The tyrannosaurus walked on two legs. It was an enormous carnivore. It was about 12 metres long and almost six metres tall. It was very strong and it could run very fast. It had 60 sharp teeth. Its teeth were very big – about the same size as bananas.

Diplodocus

The diplodocus walked on four legs. It was a herbivore. It had a very long neck so that it could eat leaves from the top of tall trees. It also had a very long tail so that it could balance. It couldn't run very fast.

Triceratops

The triceratops was a herbivore. It had three horns and a large frill around its neck. Scientists think that it used its horns for protection against dangerous predators, for example the tyrannosaurus. Its nose and mouth were like a beak. It was nine metres long and three metres tall.

The longest dinosaur name is MICROPACHYCEPHALOSAURUS. CAN YOU SAY IT?

After you read

Go to page 31 in your Activity Book.

Key learning outcomes: read and understand an information text

Text type: **an encyclopaedia entry**

Investigate a text

1 **Look at the picture. Which words do you think describe a stegosaurus?** Whole Class

fast slow herbivore carnivore shiny tiny enormous friendly

2 **Read and listen to find out.** CD2 09

Reading tip!
Use the diagram to help you understand the new words in the text.

Stegosaurus

The stegosaurus lived about 150 million years ago. It was an enormous herbivore. It was nine metres long. It walked on four legs. It couldn't run very fast. It had spikes on its tail and large, shiny plates on its back. It had small, flat teeth at the back of its beak. The stegosaurus had a tiny head. Its brain was about the same size as a small orange!

Discuss a text

3 **Think and discuss.** Whole Class

1 Does the encyclopaedia entry contain facts or personal opinions?

2 What information does it give about the stegosaurus?

3 Are there any labelled illustrations?

4 What adjectives can you find in the text?

Writing tip!
We don't use ***very*** with extreme adjectives.

*It was an **enormous** herbivore.*	***Enormous*** *means* **very big.**
*The stegosaurus had a **tiny** head.*	***Tiny*** *means* **very small.**

Plan and write an encyclopaedia entry on page 32 in your Activity Book.

1 Read Luke's questions. What do you think?

Whole Class

I'm at a special place in **Canada** called Dinosaur Provincial Park. Can you answer these questions?

1 What's Dinosaur Provincial Park famous for?

2 How many different species of dinosaurs did scientists find there?

3 How can you tell the difference between a rock and a bone?

4 What do the cave paintings in Writing-on-Stone Provincial Park show us?

2 Read and listen. Answer Luke's questions.

CD2 10

dinosaur fossils in Canada

DINOSAUR DISCOVERIES in Canada

Alberta, in Canada, is home to many beautiful parks. You can see lots of amazing wildlife and scenery in these parks, but some of them are also famous for exciting discoveries.

Dinosaur Provincial Park in Alberta, is famous for its dinosaur fossils. Scientists found fossils of more than 40 different species of dinosaurs here. Some of them are more than 75 million years old!

If you want to find out what it's like to be a palaeontologist, you can go on a fossil safari. Here, you can learn some of the secrets of discovering and identifying fossils. Did you know that one way of telling the difference between a bone and a rock is to lick your finger and touch the rock? If it sticks to your finger, it's a bone.

Dinosaur Provincial Park is also famous for its beautiful scenery. You can go hiking along the paths where dinosaurs once walked, and you can even go camping.

PALAEONTOLOGIST
= a person who studies fossils

*Also in Alberta, you can visit **Writing-on-Stone Provincial Park**. Here, you can see cave paintings and carvings on the rocks that are over 3000 years old! They were made by tribes who lived here in the past. They show us how people lived thousands of years ago.*

Think about your culture Are there any dinosaur fossils in your country? Which dinosaurs are they from? Are there any cave paintings or carvings in your country?

Do the Canada web quest and the Unit Review on pages 33 and 34 in your Activity Book. ICT

Key learning outcomes: read about dinosaur fossils in Canada; think about and research Canada

Today's programme is about museums. Do you like going to museums?

1 **Watch the video. What can a museum tell you about these things?**

2 **Watch the video again. Read and answer the questions.**

1 What can you see in the Natural History Museum?

2 When did dinosaurs live?

3 How did Egyptian people write?

4 What did people paint in caves?

5 What did archaeologists find?

3 **What can you find out about these things in a virtual museum?** ICT

Exploring virtual museums

You can take a tour of a museum online. There are a lot of virtual museums around the world you can visit!

1

dinosaurs

2

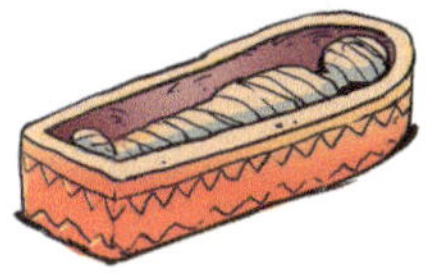

mummies

3

cave men

4

fossils

Key learning outcomes: watch and understand a video about museums

21st **Digital skills:** exploring virtual museums

The minibeast exhibition

Design a minibeast exhibition for a natural history museum and give a presentation.

Investigate

1 Is there a natural history museum in your town? What exhibitions can you visit? What can you see in the exhibitions? Whole Class

2 Talk Partners Work in groups. Look at the minibeast exhibition and make lists.

- List the minibeasts that have got six legs.
- List the minibeasts that can fly.
- List four things you can see in the animals' living areas.

3 Listen and check your lists. Listen again and repeat the words. CD2 14

4 Choose three minibeasts and find out more. Make notes on page 36 in your Activity Book.

Digital tip!
Use the Internet to investigate your minibeasts.

Key learning outcomes: learn about exhibitions in your town museum; investigate different minibeasts **Language:** minibeasts and their habitats

Plan and create your project

1 **Talk Partners** **Discuss the questions. Write the information on page 37 in your Activity Book.**

1 What's the name of the exhibition? *The exhibition is called …*

2 Which minibeasts are in the exhibition? Choose eight. *There are some dragonflies, …*

3 What do your minibeasts need? *The dragonflies need a pond, …*

4 How are you going to organise the exhibition? *I'm going to put all the minibeasts that can fly next to each other.*

Cooperative learning **Listen to and respect everyone's opinion.**

2 **Design and draw your minibeast exhibition.**

- Draw the tanks ✔
- Draw the minibeasts ✔
- Write the labels ✔

Present your project

3 **Present your minibeast exhibition to the class.**

Think about your project

Go to page 37 in your Activity Book.

Key learning outcomes: work in a group to create a minibeast exhibition; present the exhibition to the class **Language:** *We can have some dragonflies. The dragonflies need a pond.*

Unit 4 Lost in space

1 What's in the sky? What can you see during the day? What can you see at night? Make two lists. Brainstorm ???

2 Listen, point and say the vocabulary chant. CD2 15

3 Listen, look and sing *In our solar system*. CD2 16

There are planets
And asteroids,
Comets and moons,
In our solar system.

Mercury is the first planet.
It's the closest planet to the Sun.
Venus is the second planet.
It's the hottest planet of them all.
Chorus

Earth is the third planet.
It's the planet where we live.
Mars is the fourth planet.
Then there's the asteroid belt.
Chorus

Jupiter is the fifth planet.
It's the biggest planet of them all.
Saturn is the sixth planet.
It's got lots of rings.
Chorus

Uranus is the seventh planet.
It's the coldest planet of them all.
Neptune is the eighth planet.
It's the furthest planet from the Sun.
Chorus

4 Talk Partners **Play a guessing game.**

It's next to Earth. It's the fourth planet.

Is it Mars?

Yes, it is. Well done.

1 planets

2 comet

3 Mercury

4 Venus

5 Neptune

6 Jupiter

7 meteorite

8 rocket

9 astronaut

10 satellite

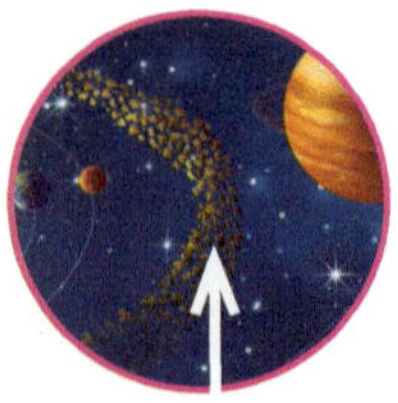
11 asteroid belt

12 rings

Key learning outcomes: identify and say objects in space; sing a song about the solar system
Vocabulary: objects in space

1 Listen and read. Listen and repeat. Act out.

CD2 18

Josh: This model of the solar system is great. Did you make it?

Ravi: Yes, I did. I made it with my dad. He told me a lot about the planets.

Josh: Which planet is this?

Ravi: It's Jupiter. Jupiter is the biggest planet.

Josh: Which planet is this?

Ravi: It's Mercury. Mercury is the closest planet to the Sun.

Josh: Cool! Which is the hottest planet?

Ravi: Venus is the hottest planet.

Josh: I know this planet. It's Earth. Earth is the best planet.

Ravi: Yes, because it's where we live!

2 Read again. Which planets does Josh not know?

3 Listen and follow. Repeat.

CD2 19

Superlative adjectives: short adjectives

Venus		the **hottest**	
Uranus		the **coldest**	
Jupiter	is	the **biggest**	planet.
Mercury		the **smallest**	
		the **closest**	planet to the Sun.
Neptune		the **furthest**	from the Sun.

4 Talk Partners

Make true sentences.

Mercury is the closest planet to the Sun.

Uranus is the coldest planet.

Grammar clue

We add -est to short adjectives to make the superlative small **– smallest**

We double the final letter of some adjectives before adding -est big **– biggest**

Some adjectives are irregular

good – better **– best** bad – worse **– worst**

Key learning outcomes: use superlative adjectives to talk about the planets

Grammar: *Jupiter is the biggest planet.*

Before you read

1 **Use the code to read the message from Luke.**

Last night, I looked at the stars with my telescope.
I saw a 195-637-501-245-783.

What do you think the children see in the night sky?

2 **Listen and read. Act out.** CD2 20

The meteorite

Key learning outcomes: read, listen and understand a story about a meteorite
Language: *What was that? It was a meteorite.*

After you read

3 **Talk Partners** **Ask and answer.**

1 Which is the closest planet to Earth?

Venus is the closest planet to Earth.

2 Where does the meteorite fall?

3 What do Josh and Lily find?

4 What does Lily want to do?

5 Do the children find the meteorite?

4 **Values** **Read and discuss.** Whole Class

- Did the children do the right thing with the starfish?
- What can happen to living things out of their habitats?
- How can you help animals that are out of their habitats?
- How can we protect animals in the environment?

Values: don't take living things out of their habitats

1 Listen, point and say. CD2 22

1 shiny

2 expensive

3 modern

4 heavy

5 powerful

6 interesting

2 Listen and sing *The best rocket in the world*. CD2 23

I made a rocket all by myself.
It's the best rocket
In the world.

It's the shiniest rocket,
The most modern rocket.
It's the greatest rocket
In the world.
Chorus

It's the most powerful rocket,
The most expensive rocket.
It's the fastest rocket
In the world.
Chorus

It's the heaviest rocket,
The most interesting rocket.
It's the most fantastic rocket
In the world.
Chorus

3 Listen and follow. Repeat. CD2 24

Superlative adjectives: long adjectives

The red rocket		the heaviest	
The blue rocket		the shiniest	
The purple rocket	is	the most interesting	rocket.
The green rocket		the most powerful	
The black rocket		the most expensive	
The orange rocket		the most modern	

4 Talk Partners Play a *true* or *false* game.

The orange rocket is the most modern.

That's true.

Grammar clue

We take away the *-y* from the adjective and add -iest to make the superlative.

shiny – **shiniest** heavy – **heaviest**

We add *most* to long adjectives.

Key learning outcomes: identify and say adjectives; use short and long superlative adjectives
Vocabulary: adjectives **Grammar:** *The purple rocket is the most interesting rocket.*

1 Listen, read and say. CD2 25

A horse and a snake had a race in space. The snake came eighth and the horse said 'neigh' and went away on a sleigh.

Now practise spelling on page 42 in your Activity Book.

2 Read the rocket cards. Listen and say *true* or *false*. CD2 26

Cosmic Comet

Weight:	750kg
Height:	6m
Price:	£30,000
Date of manufacture:	1990
Engine power:	4
Interest rating:	★ ★

Moon Raider

Weight:	700kg
Height:	9m
Price:	£20,000
Date of manufacture:	1975
Engine power:	5
Interest rating	★

Red Rocket

Weight:	550kg
Height:	11m
Price:	£25,000
Date of manufacture:	1985
Engine power:	3
Interest rating	★ ★ ★

3 Talk Partners Ask and answer about the rockets.

Teacher's Resource Bank: Unit 4

Key learning outcomes: listen for specific information; play a communication game using superlative adjectives **Phonics:** Alternative vowel spellings: *a_e – eigh*

Before you read

1 Look at the title and the subheadings in the fact file. What do you think the gas giants are? What do you already know about the gas giants? Whole Class

2 Read and listen. Find the answers to these questions. CD2 27

Which planet has got the biggest moon? Which is the windiest planet?

Which planet has got the brightest rings?

Which is the coldest planet?

Reading tip!
Read the subheadings first to give you clues about the text.

THE GAS GIANTS

Jupiter, Saturn, Uranus and Neptune are the four planets furthest from the Sun. They're known as the gas giants.

Jupiter

Distance from the Sun: *It's the fifth planet from the Sun.*
Size: *It's the biggest planet.*
Rings: *It's got three rings.*
Moons: *It's got at least 16 moons. One of its moons is the biggest moon in the solar system.*
Interesting information: *It's the heaviest planet. The large red spot on Jupiter is a storm that started at least 400 years ago.*

Saturn

Distance from the Sun: *It's the sixth planet from the Sun.*
Size: *It's the second biggest planet.*
Rings: *It's got thousands of rings made of ice and rock. Saturn's rings are the brightest rings in the solar system.*
Moons: *It's got at least 30 moons. It's the planet with the most moons.*
Interesting information: *Some of the pieces of ice in Saturn's rings are as big as a house.*

Uranus

Distance from the Sun: *It's the seventh planet from the Sun.*
Size: *It's the third biggest planet.*
Rings: *It's got 11 grey rings.*
Moons: *It's got at least 22 moons.*
Interesting information: *It's the coldest planet.*

Neptune

Distance from the Sun: *It's the furthest planet from the Sun.*
Size: *It's the fourth biggest planet.*
Rings: *It's got four complete rings made of rock and dust, and lots of incomplete rings.*
Moons: *It's got at least eight moons.*
Interesting information: *It's the windiest planet.*

After you read

Go to page 43 in your Activity Book.

Text type: **a fact file**

Investigate a text

1 Look at the photos in the fact file. Think of questions to ask about Mars. Whole Class

2 Read and listen. Can you find the answers to your questions in the fact file? CD2 28

Mars

Surface:
Mars is known as the red planet because its surface is covered with red dust. It's a dry, rocky planet, but scientists believe that there was once water on Mars. Now, it's got ice caps at its north and south poles, just like Earth.

Mountains:
The highest mountains in the solar system are on Mars. Mars has also got the largest volcano in the solar system. It's called Mount Olympus.

Moons:
Mars has got two moons. They're shaped like potatoes!

Interesting information:
Mars is a cold planet. The average temperature on Mars is -23ºC.

Discuss a text

3 Think and discuss. Whole Class

1 Does the fact file contain facts or personal opinions?

2 Is the fact file divided into sections?

3 Are there subheadings in the fact file?

4 Is the information in alphabetical order?

Writing tip!

Information is easier to understand if we divide it into sections. We can give each section a subheading.

Find the subheadings in the Mars fact file.

Plan and write a fact file about Earth on page 44 in your Activity Book.

Key learning outcomes: prepare and write a fact file; use subheadings

1 **Read Luke's questions. What do you think?** Whole Class

I'm in **Australia** now, looking at the stars and planets through an amazing telescope.
Can you answer these questions?

1 What's the sky like at the Siding Spring Observatory?

2 How many telescopes are there?

3 What are nebulas?

4 What can you see if you drive away from the observatory?

2 **Read and listen. Answer Luke's questions.** CD2 29

observatories in Australia

Siding Spring Observatory

At the Siding Spring Observatory in Australia, scientists and astronomers look at stars, planets, asteroids and comets in the night sky. The sky in this area is great for stargazing. It's very dark and clean, away from the smoke and pollution of the city. The best place for an observatory is away from towns and cities. You need clear skies and a high position.

There are 12 telescopes at the Siding Spring Observatory. It's the largest observatory in Australia, and astronomers come from all over the world to study the sky here. They use the powerful telescopes to see nebulas. These are clouds of dust and gas where new stars are born.

The largest telescope at the observatory is the Anglo-Australian telescope. Visitors can look inside this telescope during the day, to see how the astronomers work.

The people at the Siding Spring Observatory have created a tour of the solar system for us to explore … by car! The Anglo-Australian telescope represents the Sun. If you get in your car and drive away from the telescope, you can see models of the planets, in order of their distance from the Sun. The first planet you can see is Mercury. Which planet do you think is the furthest from the Anglo-Australian telescope?

Think about your culture Are there any observatories in your country? Can you visit them? Can you see any stars from your bedroom window?

Do the Australia web quest and the Unit Review on pages 45 and 46 in your Activity Book. ICT

Key learning outcomes: read about an observatory in Australia; think about and research Australia

21 CHANNEL

Today's programme is about space. What's your favourite planet? Why?

1 **Watch the video. Which planets are these?**

2 **Watch the video again. Read and say *true* or *false*. Correct the false sentences.**

1 All the planets are made of rock.
2 Venus is the coldest planet.
3 Jupiter is the biggest and heaviest planet.
4 Saturn has got the brightest rings in the Solar System.
5 Mars is the nearest planet to the Sun.

3 **Work with your partner. Can you put these planets in order? Look, think and say.**

Grading things

Using a cline can help us put things in order.

1
Venus
Neptune
Mars
hot
cold

2
Jupiter
Venus
Saturn
big
small

3
Mercury
Neptune
Earth
far
close

Unit 5 Let's have fun!

1 **What activities do you do in your free time? Make a list. What's your favourite activity? What did you do last weekend?** Brainstorm

2 **Listen, point and say the vocabulary chant.** CD2 33

3 **Listen, look and sing *What shall we do today?*** CD2 34

1 go sailing

2 go bowling

3 have an ice lolly

4 have a picnic

5 go shopping

6 go hiking

7 make a cake

8 go windsurfing

9 play table tennis

10 go horse riding

11 ride a mountain bike

12 have a barbecue

What shall we do today?
What shall we do today?
Let's go hiking!
Let's go bowling!
Let's have a barbecue!
Let's have a picnic!
Let's go sailing!
There are so many things to do.
Chorus
Let's go shopping!
Let's play table tennis!
Let's ride a mountain bike!
Let's have an ice lolly!
Let's make a cake!
There are so many things we like.
Chorus

4 **Talk Partners** **Play a mime game.**

What do you do at the weekend? Do you go bowling?

No, I don't.

Do you play table tennis?

Yes, I do.

Key learning outcomes: identify and say free-time activities; sing a song about free-time activities
Vocabulary: free-time activities

1 **Listen and read. Listen and repeat. Act out.** CD2 35

Josh: That was great fun!

Lily: What can we do tomorrow?

Josh: If it's windy, we can go windsurfing on the lake.

Lily: Oh yes! And if it's sunny, we can have a barbecue in the afternoon.

Josh: But we can't have a barbecue if it's wet.

Lily: You're right. I know. If it's raining, we can go bowling.

Josh: What a good idea. I love bowling!

Lily: Me too.

2 **Read again. What can Josh and Lily do tomorrow?**

3 **Listen and follow. Repeat.** CD2 36

Conditional with *can*

	raining,		**go shopping.**
	wet,		**make a cake.**
If it's	**sunny,**	**we can**	**have a picnic.**
	hot,	**we can't**	**ride a mountain bike.**
	windy,		**play table tennis.**
	dry,		**watch TV.**

4 **Talk Partners**

Make true sentences.

If it's hot, we can have a picnic.

If it's wet, we can't ride a mountain bike.

Grammar clue

Conditional sentences with *can / can't* have got two parts.

If + present simple, we can + verb.

We can change the order of the two parts (but we don't use a comma).

We **can go windsurfing if it's** windy.

Key learning outcomes: use conditional sentences with *can*

Grammar: *If it's sunny, we can have a picnic.*

Before you read

1 **Use the code to read the message from Luke.**

When I was in Australia, I bought a 231–389–231–311–245–715–389–231–637–637. I'm learning to play it. If you're bored, you can play the instruments in my bedroom.

Read the title of the story. What activities can the children do if it's raining?

2 **Listen and read. Act out.** CD2 37

The rainy day

Key learning outcomes: read, listen and understand a story about a rainy day
Language: *Do you want to play the tambourine? I'd rather play the drums.*

After you read

3 **Talk Partners** **Ask and answer.**

1 Can they ride their mountain bikes? Why?

> No, they can't. It's raining.

2 What do the children decide to do?

3 What does Lily play at school?

4 How do the children make the xylophone?

5 Who do they send a video to?

4 **Values** **Read and discuss.** Whole Class

- Are the children disappointed because they can't ride their mountain bikes?
- Are they creative with their time?
- What can you do if it's raining?
- Are you creative with your time?

1 Listen, point and say. CD2 39

1 drums

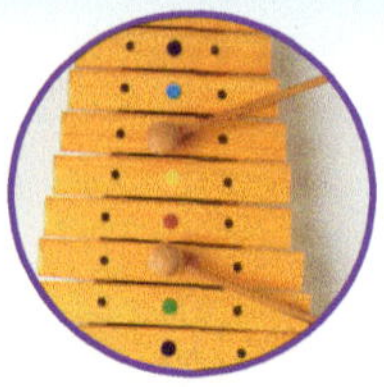
2 xylophone

3 keyboard

4 cymbals

5 tambourine

6 electric guitar

2 Listen and sing *I'd rather sing*. CD2 40

I love playing the drums.
I like the xylophone.
I want to be in a rock band,
But I'd rather sing.
I'd rather sing than play the drums.
I'd rather sing than play the xylophone.
I love playing instruments,
But I'd rather sing.

I'd rather sing, I'd rather sing,
I'd rather sing, I'd rather sing.

I love playing the cymbals.
I like the tambourine.
I want to be in a rock band,
But I'd rather sing.
I'd rather sing than play the cymbals.
I'd rather sing than play the tambourine.
I love playing instruments,
But I'd rather sing.

I'd rather sing, I'd rather sing,
I'd rather sing, I'd rather sing.

3 Listen and follow. Repeat. CD2 42

would rather

		the drums		
		the xylophone		
I'd rather	play	the keyboard	than	sing.
		the cymbals		
		the tambourine		
		the electric guitar		

Grammar clue

We can use I'd rather to talk about preferences. We can also ask questions.
Would you rather play the keyboard or sing?
I'd rather play the keyboard than sing.

Remember!
I'd = I would

4 Talk Partners Ask and answer.

Would you rather play the cymbals or sing?

I'd rather play the cymbals than sing.

Key learning outcomes: identify and say musical instruments; use *I'd rather* to talk about preferences
Vocabulary: musical instruments **Grammar:** *Would you rather play the cymbals or sing? I'd rather sing.*

1 Listen, read and say. CD2 43

Speak and spell

→ Now practise spelling on page 52 in your Activity Book.

2 Read the questionnaire. Listen and identify five differences. CD2 44

Free-time questionnaire

Name: Holly Williams

Age: 10

Address: 15 Church Road

Would you rather …

make a cake	✔	eat an ice lolly	☐
go shopping	☐	go bowling	✔
have a picnic	☐	have a barbecue	✔
go horse riding	✔	ride a mountain bike	☐
go windsurfing	☐	go sailing	✔

3 → **Talk Partners** Ask and answer to complete the questionnaire. Tell a friend.

Teacher's Resource Bank: Unit 5

Key learning outcomes: listen for specific information; play a communication game using *would rather* **Phonics:** Alternative vowel spellings: *u_e – ue*

Literacy

Before you read

1 **Which of these things do you think will be in a myth?** Whole Class

music a monster a princess a hero a mountain bike sailors

2 **Look at the pictures. What do you think Sirens are?** Whole Class

3 **Read and listen to find out. What do the Sirens do?** CD2 45

Ulysses and the Sirens

The Odyssey is a poem from Ancient Greece. It's about Ulysses and his adventures as he travels home after a war. On the way, Ulysses must pass the Sirens' island on his ship.

The Sirens were mythical creatures. They were part woman and part bird. They lived on a rocky island in the middle of the sea. They sang the most beautiful songs. Sailors wanted to listen to the songs. Sometimes, sailors jumped into the sea when they heard the songs, and their ships crashed into the rocks. Nobody could pass the Sirens' island without disaster.

Ulysses told the sailors on his ship to put wax in their ears. With wax in their ears, the sailors couldn't hear the Sirens singing. Ulysses didn't put wax in his ears because he wanted to hear the songs. He asked his sailors to tie him to the ship's mast so he couldn't jump off the ship.

When the ship passed the Sirens' island, the Sirens started singing. The sailors couldn't hear the songs. Ulysses could hear the songs, but he couldn't jump off the ship. The ship sailed safely past the island. The sailors untied Ulysses and removed the wax from their ears.

Ulysses was the only person to hear the Sirens' song and live to tell the tale.

After you read

Go to page 53 in your Activity Book.

Key learning outcomes: read and understand a text to entertain

Text type: **a myth / a mythical creature**

Investigate a text

1 **The Sirens are mythical creatures. What do you remember about them?**

Where did they live? What did they look like? What did they do?

2 **Do you know any other mythical creatures?**

3 **Read and listen. What was a Hydra? How many heads did it have?** CD2 46

Reading tip!

Look at the picture of the Hydra. Describe it with your partner before you read the text.

THE HYDRA

The Hydra was an enormous, poisonous snake.
It looked like a dragon.
The Hydra lived in a swamp and ate people
from the village and their cows.
It was nine metres tall.
It had four legs. It had nine heads and 18
terrible eyes! It could grow new heads, too.
The Hydra's claws and breath were poisonous.

Discuss a text

4 **Think and discuss.**

What information does the text give us about …

- the Hydra's appearance?
- the Hydra's diet?
- the Hydra's size?
- the Hydra's habitat?

Writing tip!

We use an **apostrophe** followed by **s** to show possession.

The Hydra's claws and breath were poisonous.

When something belongs to more than one person, we only use an **apostrophe**.

… the Sirens' island … *… the Sirens' song …*

Invent and write about a mythical creature on page 54 in your Activity Book.

1 **Read Luke's questions. What do you think?** Whole Class

I'm in **New Zealand** for the WOMAD music festival. There are instruments from all over the world here. Can you answer these questions?

1 What are bagpipes made from?
2 Which instrument comes from Trinidad and Tobago?
3 What's a didgeridoo made from?
4 What's the sitar like?

2 **Read and listen. Answer Luke's questions.** CD3 01

music festivals in New Zealand

WOMAD

WOMAD (World of Music, Arts and Dance) is a music and dance festival that started in 1982. There are WOMAD festivals in countries all over the world, including New Zealand, Australia, Russia and Britain. In New Zealand, people come from all over the world to listen to music and to dance. The performers bring instruments from lots of different countries.

BAGPIPES are the national instrument of Scotland. They have a bag and one or more pipes. The pipes are made from wood. The bag is usually made from animal skin. Many years ago, Scottish people used bagpipes to help motivate soldiers in wars.

The **STEEL DRUM**, or steel pan, is made from recycled metal containers. It's the national instrument of Trinidad and Tobago. People play steel pans in steel bands. Some steel bands have got 100 musicians!

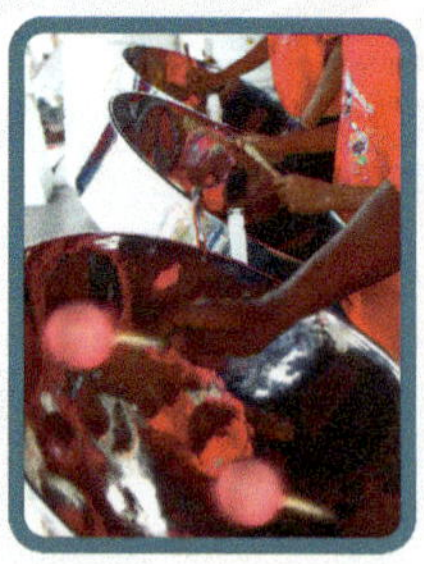

The **DIDGERIDOO** comes from Australia. It's probably the world's oldest instrument. It's made from the trunk or branch of a tree. To play a didgeridoo, you blow into the top and a noise comes out of the bottom.

The **SITAR** is a popular instrument from India. It looks like a guitar. It's got a long neck and it's got about 20 strings. To play the sitar, you sit on the floor with the bottom of the sitar resting on your foot.

Think about your culture **Are there any music festivals in your country? What traditional instruments do people play in your country? Do you play an instrument?**

Do the New Zealand web quest and the Unit Review on pages 55 and 56 in your Activity Book. ICT

Key learning outcomes: read about WOMAD in New Zealand; think about and research New Zealand

21 CHANNEL

Today's programme is about free time activities. What do you do in your free time?

1 Watch the video. Which free time activities use these objects?

1 
2 
3 
4 
5 

2 Watch the video again. Read and answer the questions.

1 When can you go to the park?
2 What are the girls cooking?
3 What do the boys use to build their city?
4 What do you need to wear to do an experiment?
5 Can you play table tennis inside?

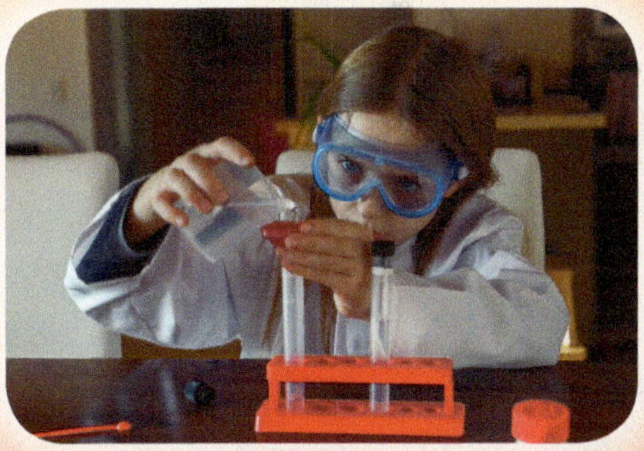

3 Read and answer. What activities can you do in different weather conditions?

Making your own fun

Try to find different ways of making your own fun!

1 What can you do if it's sunny?

2 What can you do if it's raining?

3 What can you do if it's windy?

4 What can you do if it's snowing?

Key learning outcomes: watch and understand a video about free-time activities
21st **Living in the world:** making your own fun

Unit 6 Marvellous machines

1 washing machine

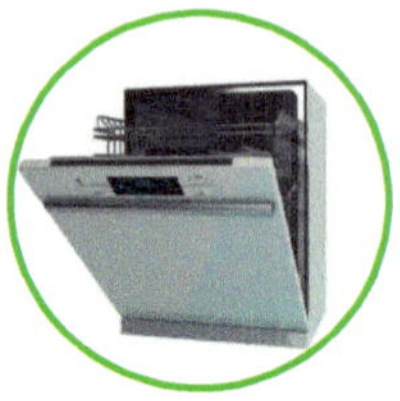

2 dishwasher

3 toaster

4 cooker

5 DVD player

6 blender

7 hairdryer

8 printer

9 microwave

10 fridge

11 tablet

12 hoover

1 **What machines are there in your house? Make a list. Where can you find each machine?** Brainstorm

2 **Listen, point and say the vocabulary chant.** CD3 05

3 **Listen, look and sing *Our house*.** CD3 06

Our house is full of machines,
Upstairs and downstairs, too.
We've got machines in the kitchen,
In the bedroom and in the living room.
There's a cooker in the kitchen.
We use it for cooking food.
There's a fridge in the kitchen, too.
It keeps everything cool.
Chorus

There's a hairdryer in the bedroom.
We use it for drying our hair.
The DVD player is in the living room.
We watch DVDs there.
Chorus

There's a dishwasher in the kitchen.
We use it for washing dirty plates.
There's a blender in the kitchen, too.
We use it for making cakes.
Chorus

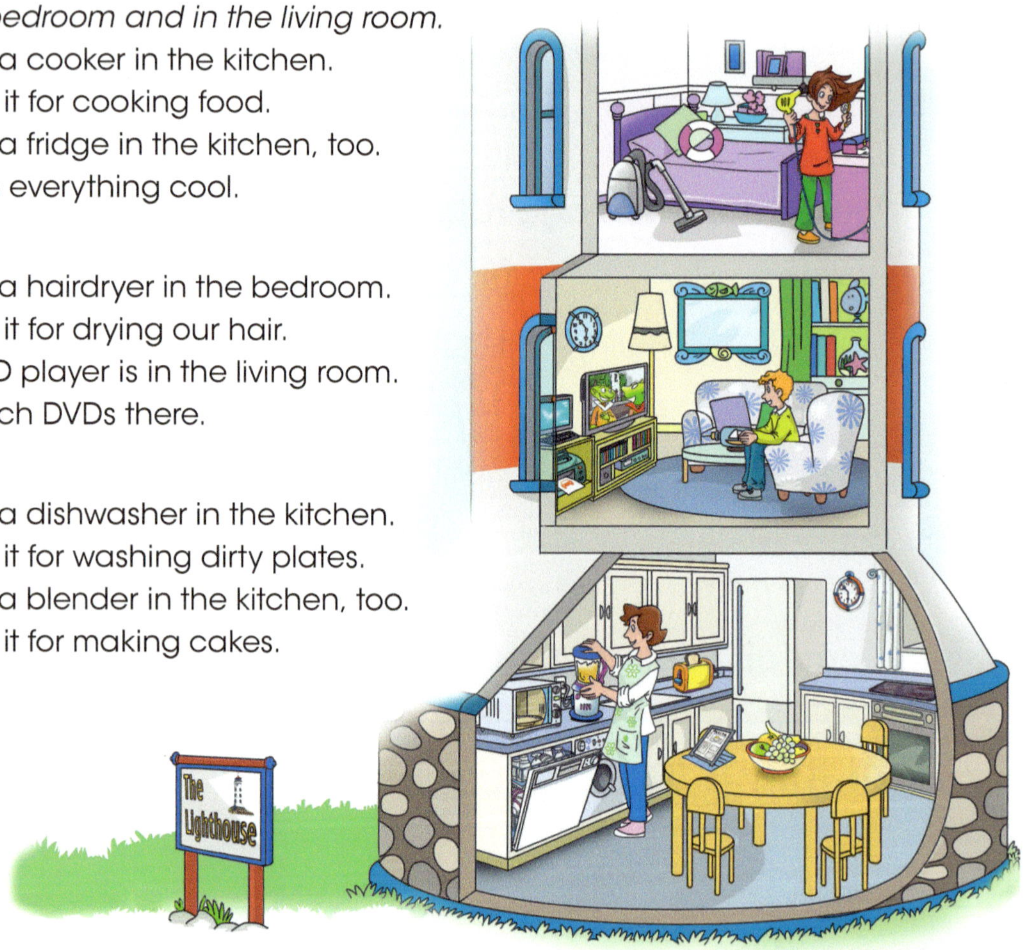

4 **Talk Partners** **Ask and answer.**

Have you got a dishwasher?

Yes, I have.

Where is it?

It's in the kitchen.

How often do you use it?

I use it every day.

Key learning outcomes: identify and say machines in our houses; sing a song about machines in our houses **Vocabulary:** machines in our houses

1 **Listen and read. Listen and repeat. Act out.** CD3 08

Ravi: Hi, Lily. Where were you this morning?

Lily: I was at the shopping centre with my mum and dad.

Ravi: What did you buy?

Lily: Can you guess? It's a machine. It's used for heating food.

Ravi: Is it a microwave?

Lily: Yes, it is. Well done!

Ravi: Did you buy anything else?

Lily: Yes, I did. It's used for drying your hair.

Ravi: A hairdryer!

2 **Read again. What did Lily buy?**

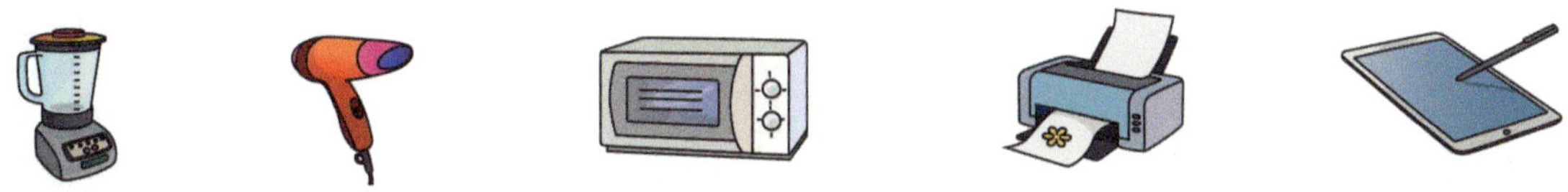

3 **Listen and follow. Repeat.** CD3 09

used for

A fridge			**keeping food cold.**
A washing machine			**washing your clothes.**
A toaster	**is**	**used for**	**making toast.**
Microwaves	**are**		**heating food.**
Hairdryers			**drying your hair.**
DVD players			**watching DVDs.**

4 **Talk Partners**

Play a *true or false* game.

Toasters are used for watching DVDs.

That's false.

Grammar clue

We say that something is or things are used for + -ing.

A washing machine **is used for washing** your clothes.

Toasters **are used for making** toast.

Key learning outcomes: use *is / are used for* to talk about machines in our houses

Grammar: *A toaster is used for making toast.*

Before you read

1 **Use the code to read the message from Luke.**

> Yesterday, the 177-153-783-783-245-715-947 in my watch stopped!

Read the title of the story. What type of boats do you think are in the race?

2 **Listen and read. Act out.** CD3 10

The boat race

Key learning outcomes: read, listen and understand a story about a boat race **Language:** *What's wrong with the boat? Why isn't it moving? We can make a battery out of lemons.*

After you read

3 **Talk Partners** **Read and correct.**

1 Josh made the boat.

No, he didn't. Ravi made the boat

2 Ravi brings four batteries for the boat.

3 The sail helps the boat move.

4 The battery is made of oranges.

5 The children win the race.

4 **Values** **Read and discuss.** Whole Class

- What do you think the children do with the old batteries at the end of the race?
- What do you do with batteries that don't work?
- Where can you recycle batteries?
- What else can you recycle?

1 Listen, point and say. CD3 12

1 wool

2 cotton

3 leather

4 plastic

5 gold

6 silver

2 Listen and sing *What's it made of?* CD3 13

This is my new sweater.
It's very warm.
What's it made of?
It's made of wool.
I love it!

This is my new bracelet.
It's very shiny.
What's it made of?
It's made of silver.
I love it!

These are my new boots.
They're very soft.
What are they made of?
They're made of leather.
I love them!

3 Listen and follow. Repeat. CD3 14

made of

A sweater			**wool.**
A bracelet			**gold.**
A T-shirt	is	made of	**cotton.**
Boots	are		**leather.**
Earrings			**silver.**
Bottles			**plastic.**

Grammar clue

What**'s** a sweater made of? **It's** made of wool.
What **are** boots made of? **They're** made of leather.

4 Talk Partners Make true sentences.

It's made of wool.

Is it a sweater?

Yes, it is.

It's my turn. They're made of leather.

Are they boots?

No, they aren't. Try again.

Key learning outcomes: identify and say materials; use *It's* and *They're* to talk about what materials things are made of **Vocabulary:** materials **Grammar:** *It's made of (gold). They're made of (leather).*

1 Listen, read and say. CD3 15

Speak and spell

'o_e' or 'o'?

The robot rolls home with a rose and hits its nose on a phone.

Now practise spelling on page 62 in your Activity Book.

Listening tip!
Follow the path with your finger as you listen.

2 Look at the chart. Listen and say *true* or *false*. CD3 16

- **big**
  - **plastic**
    - sitting on
    - drying your hair
  - **leather**
    - carrying things
    - protecting your feet
- **small**
  - **silver**
    - decorating your neck
    - decorating your ears
  - **wool**
    - keeping your head warm
    - keeping your hands warm

3 **Talk Partners** Ask and answer to find out your friend's objects.

Teacher's Resource Bank: Unit 6

Key learning outcomes: listen for specific information; play a communication game using *It's made of* and *They're made of* **Phonics:** Alternative vowel spellings: *o_e – o*

Before you read

1. Where can you see adverts? What can you see adverts for? What do adverts do? *Whole Class*
2. Look at the picture. What do you think this advert is for? *Whole Class*
3. Read and listen to find out. CD3 17

After you read

Go to page 63 in your Activity Book.

Key learning outcomes: read and understand a text to persuade

Text type: **an advert**

Investigate a text

1. Look at the pictures. What are the adverts for? *Whole Class*
2. Read and listen. Which advert do you think is better? Why? CD3 18

Discuss a text

3. Think and discuss. *Whole Class*

Find these things in the MixerTronic advert:

- a slogan
- the price
- a true statement
- the product name
- *wow* words
- an opinion
- a special offer
- photos

Writing tip!

We can use **wow words** to make texts more exciting.

incredible | *exciting* | *amazing* | *fantastic* | *delicious*

Plan and write an advert in your Activity Book (page 64).

Key learning outcomes: prepare and write an advert; use wow words

1 **Read Luke's questions. What do you think?** Whole Class

Last week, I went to see RoboGames in California, in the **USA**. Every year, people bring the best robots to compete. Can you answer these questions?

1 How many different competitions are there at RoboGames?
2 What can the robots do?
3 Are all of the robots controlled by humans?
4 What are the robots made of?

2 **Read and listen. Answer Luke's questions.** CD3 19

robot competitions

ROBOGAMES

RoboGames is a very important robot competition. People come to California, in the USA, to compete in over 50 different competitions. There are firefighting robots, robots that play hockey and football, and even robots that do kung fu. Teams come from 19 different countries to compete for gold, silver and bronze medals.

There are robot dogs, too. These amazing little machines can wag their tails and do tricks. The robot dogs play football together, too.

The robots are very clever. Some can climb stairs, do martial arts, perform somersaults and do breakdancing. The robots don't just play games and do sports, though. They're carefully designed and made so that they can see, balance and find things on their own. Some of the robots can even get out of mazes! Not all of the robots are controlled by humans – most of them do it all on their own. They're amazing!

It can take a very long time to build a robot, and they can be very expensive to build. The robots are made of many different types of materials. Some are made of new materials and others are made of recycled materials.

Think about your culture **Are there any robot competitions where you live? What do the robots do? What are robots used for in your country?**

Do the USA web quest and the Unit Review on pages 65 and 66 in your Activity Book. ICT

Key learning outcomes: read about a robot competition in the USA; think about and research the USA

Today's programme is about the power of adverts. Do you watch adverts?

1 **Watch the video. Which things are advertised in the video?**

2 **Watch the video again. Read and say *true* or *false*. Correct the false sentences.**

1 The skateboard is expensive.

2 The cars are made of metal and rubber.

3 The planes are made of metal.

4 The badminton game is on special offer.

5 The seagull is solar-powered.

3 **Think and say. How can you advertise these products? Look at Activity 1 on page 67 in your Activity Book.**

Creating adverts

Use *wow* words to make your product sound interesting.

1 

2 

3 

4 

Key learning outcomes: watch and understand a video about adverts

21st **Digital skills:** creating adverts

The green school project

Investigate ways of saving energy. Create an action plan to make your school green.

Investigate

1 Is your school green? Is there a recycling programme? Do you save energy at school? Whole Class

2 Talk Partners Work in groups. Look at the school and make lists.

- List four things that you can recycle.
- List three things that you can turn off.
- List three things that you can reuse.

3 Listen and check your lists. Listen again and repeat the words. CD3 23

Find out information

4 Find out about one way of making your school green. Make notes on page 68 in your Activity Book.

recycle

save electricity

save water

plant trees and plants

Key learning outcomes: learn about ways of saving energy; investigate the recycling programme in your school **Language:** ways of saving energy

Plan and create your project

1 **Discuss the questions. Design your action plan. Make notes on page 69 in your Activity Book.**

1 How can you make your school green?

I think we should save electricity.

2 Why are these action points important?

We should save electricity because …

3 How can you achieve these action points?

We can …

4 How can you tell other pupils about being green?

We can have a meeting.

Cooperative learning **Listen carefully to the speaker.**

Present your project

2 **Present your action plan to the class.**

Digital tip!

Present one idea on each slide. Use photos to illustrate your ideas.

Think about your project

Go to page 69 in your Activity Book.

Key learning outcomes: work in a group to create an action plan for making the school green; present the action plan to the class **Language:** *How can we make our school green? We should turn off the lights.*

Unit 7 In the city

1 library

2 airport

3 hotel

4 university

5 bowling alley

6 shopping centre

7 market

8 ice rink

9 art gallery

10 cinema

11 football stadium

12 adventure playground

1 **Think of places in a city. Make a list. What's your favourite place? What do you do there?** Brainstorm

2 **Listen, point and say the vocabulary chant.** CD3 24

3 **Listen, look and sing** ***I go to the city*****.** CD3 25

I go to the city at the weekend
With my dad and mum.
I see lots of places, I do lots of things,
And I have lots of fun.

Where do you go?
I go to the football stadium.
What do you do there?
I watch a football match.
Chorus

Where do you go?
I go to the ice rink.
What do you do there?
I skate on the ice.
Chorus

Where do you go?
I go to the shopping centre.
What do you buy there?
I buy some football boots.
Chorus

4 **Talk Partners** **Ask and answer.**

Where do you go at the weekend?

I usually go to the art gallery.

What do you do there?

I look at paintings and statues.

Key learning outcomes: identify and say places in a city; sing a song about the city
Vocabulary: places in a city

1 **Listen and read. Listen and repeat. Act out.** CD3 27

Lily: What are you reading, Ravi?

Ravi: It's a story about the future.

Lily: Is it interesting?

Ravi: Yes, it is. It says that cities will be different in the future.

Lily: Really? Will there be ice rinks?

Ravi: Yes, there will. It says that there will be football stadiums, too, but there won't be any airports.

Lily: Wow! That sounds interesting. Can I read it after you?

Ravi: Of course.

2 **Read again. What will there be in the future?**

3 **Listen and follow. Repeat.** CD3 28

Will there be …?

			libraries	
			hotels	
Will	there	be	ice rinks	in the future?
			universities	
			art galleries	

4 **Talk Partners**

Ask and answer about the future.

Will there be art galleries in the future?

Yes, there will.

Grammar clue

We can use short answers for questions about the future.

Will there **be** hotels in the future?

Yes, there **will**. No, there **won't**.

Key learning outcomes: use *will* to ask questions about the future and *there will* and *there won't* to answer **Grammar:** *Will there be (ice rinks) in the future? Yes, there will. No, there won't.*

Before you read

1 **Use the code to read the message from Luke.**

I'm reading a science fiction book. It's called 715-637-177-637-783 871-637-715-495-231. It's great. Do you like science fiction?

Read the title of the story. What do you think Sci-Fi City will be like?

2 **Listen and read. Act out.** CD3 29

Sci-Fi City

Key learning outcomes: read, listen and understand a story about a sci-fi city

Language: *Will there be robots in the future? Yes, there will.*

After you read

3 **Talk Partners** **Ask and answer.**

1 Does Josh think that there will be hotels on the moon in the future?

No, he doesn't.

2 Where does the alien take Josh?

3 How do they get there?

4 What will there be in the future?

5 Do you think Josh really went to Sci-Fi City?

4 **Values** **Read and discuss.** Whole Class

- Will Josh be tired the next day?
- Do you go to bed early?
- What relaxing activities can you do before you go to bed?
- Why do you think it's important to get enough sleep?

1 Listen, point and say. CD3 31

1 submarine

2 helicopter

3 hot-air balloon

4 motorbike

5 tram

6 underground

2 Listen and sing *In the future*. CD3 32

In the future, I think things will change.
I think it will be very different from today.

I think robots will drive,
And cars will fly,
And people will live on the moon.
Motorbikes will travel under the sea,
And children won't go to school.
Chorus

I think trams will have wings,
And computers will sing,
And tables will walk and books will talk.
People won't listen to the radio,
And children won't go to school.
Chorus

3 Listen and follow. Repeat. CD3 33

Future: *will*

Cars		have wings	
Robots		live on the moon	
Motorbikes	will	travel under the sea	in the future.
Submarines	won't	fly	
Computers		drive cars	
Children		go to school	

4 Talk Partners Make predictions about the future.

Cars will have wings in the future.

Children won't live on the moon in the future.

Grammar clue

We use *will* and *won't* to talk about the future.

Key learning outcomes: identify and say vocabulary about transport; use *will* and *won't* to make future predictions **Vocabulary:** transport **Grammar:** *Robots will drive. Submarines won't fly.*

1 Listen, read and say. CD3 34

Speak and spell

→ Now practise spelling on page 74 in your Activity Book.

2 Read the questionnaire. Listen and identify five differences. CD3 35

Future transport questionnaire

What do you think transport will be like in the future?

Name: Richard Thomas

Age: 11

	have wheels	fly	go to the moon	travel under the sea
submarines	✔	✗	✔	✔
helicopters	✗	✔	✗	✗
trams	✗	✗	✗	✔
hot-air balloons	✗	✔	✔	✔

3 → **Talk Partners** What do you think transport will be like in the future? Ask and answer to complete the chart.

Teacher's Resource Bank: Unit 7

Key learning outcomes: listen for specific information; play a communication game using *will / won't* **Phonics:** Alternative vowel spellings: *oy – oi*

Before you read

1 **This acrostic poem is about the future. Which of these words do you think will appear in it?** Whole Class

fossil robots cave time dinosaur machines computer

2 **Read and listen. How many of your words are in the poem?** CD3 36

After you read

Go to page 75 in your Activity Book.

Key learning outcomes: read and understand a poem

Text type: **an acrostic poem**

Investigate a text

1 **What words do you think appear in an acrostic poem about a hot-air balloon? Make a list.** Whole Class

2 **Read and listen. Can you see your words in the poem?** CD3 37

Discuss a text

3 **Think and discuss.** Whole Class

1 Where's the title of the acrostic poem?

2 Is the topic of the acrostic poem the same as the title?

3 Is the title in capital letters?

4 Do the sentences in the acrostic poem rhyme?

Writing tip!

Brainstorm words about the topic before you start writing your acrostic poem.
You can make a list or draw a mind map.
Use a dictionary to help you.

➔ **Plan and write an acrostic poem on page 76 in your Activity Book.**

Key learning outcomes: prepare and write an acrostic poem; make a list or draw a mind map to brainstorm vocabulary

1 **Read Luke's questions. What do you think?** Whole Class

I'm in **Hong Kong** now. There are lots of ways to travel around. Can you answer these questions?

1 What's a junk boat?
2 When do you pay on a tram?
3 How long does the funicular train ride take?
4 What can you see from a sampan?

2 **Read and listen. Answer Luke's questions.** CD3 38

transport in Hong Kong

TRANSPORT IN HONG KONG

Hong Kong is on the south coast of China. It's made up of islands, and it's got lots of hills, so there are many different ways of travelling around.

Junk boats

If you want to travel to different islands in Hong Kong, you can go on a tour on a junk boat. Junk boats are traditional Chinese fishing boats, which are now also used by tourists. They're made of bamboo. You can see junk boats floating in Victoria Harbour. One of the most popular boat rides is at sunset, when you can look at the beautiful scenery.

Trams

Double-decker trams travel through the streets of Hong Kong. They're very cheap. You can sit next to the window on the top deck to see great views of the city. You get on the tram at the back and you pay at the front when you get off. Make sure you have the right money!

Funicular railway

To get to the top of a big mountain in Hong Kong called The Peak, you can go on the Peak Tram. This is the steepest funicular railway in the world. This tram ride takes you to the top of the mountain in only seven minutes. From the tram, you can see all of Hong Kong below you. The view is incredible!

Sampans

Sampans are river boats. Many tourists go on 30-minute rides on sampans and explore the harbour. From the sampans, you can see the junk boats and houseboats, and even floating restaurants!

Think about your culture How do people travel in your country? What unusual forms of transport are there? Are they forms of land, sea or air transport?

Do the Hong Kong web quest and the Unit Review on pages 77 and 78 in your Activity Book. ICT

Key learning outcomes: read about transport in Hong Kong; think about and research Hong Kong

21 CHANNEL

Today's programme is about the future. What do you think life will be like in the future?

1 **Watch the video. Which of these don't you see in the video?**

2 **Watch the video again. Read and say *true* or *false*. Correct the false sentences.**

1 People think cars won't need drivers.

2 People think children will go to school by car in the future.

3 Scientists think people will deliver parcels and letters.

4 People think robots will do all the jobs in the future.

5 Cities won't be different in the future.

3 **Make predictions. Which things do you think we will have in the future?**

Making predictions

We can make predictions about the future based on the ideas we have now.

1

2

3

4

Unit 8 Jobs we do

1 chef

2 hairdresser

3 driver

4 photographer

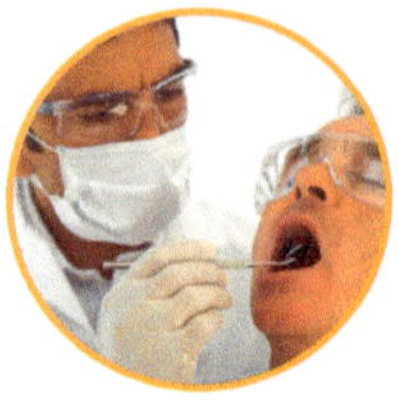

5 dentist

6 waiter

7 nurse

8 carpenter

9 mechanic

10 artist

11 lawyer

12 vet

1 **What jobs do people you know do? Make a list. What do you want to be when you're older? Why?** Brainstorm

2 **Listen, point and say the vocabulary chant.** CD3 42

3 **Listen, look and sing** ***Who is it?*** CD3 43

Who fixes your car when it doesn't work?
A mechanic.

Who cooks your food in a restaurant?
A chef.

Who takes photos for a magazine?
A photographer.

Who brings your food in a restaurant?
A waiter.

Who helps your pet when it's ill?
A vet.

Who cuts your hair when it's too long?
A hairdresser.

4 **Talk Partners** **Play a guessing game.**

This person cooks food in a restaurant.

Is it a chef?

Yes, it is.

Key learning outcomes: identify and say jobs; sing a song about jobs
Vocabulary: jobs

1 **Listen and read. Listen and repeat. Act out.** CD3 45

Josh: What do you want to be when you're older, Lily?

Lily: I want to be a vet.

Josh: Do you have to go to university to be a vet?

Lily: Yes, you do. You have to like animals, too.

Josh: I want to be a carpenter when I'm older.

Lily: Why?

Josh: Because you don't have to wear a uniform.

Lily: Of course! You love wearing jeans.

2 **Read again. Which pictures are correct?**

3 **Listen and follow. Repeat.** CD3 46

have to: questions

	I		wear a uniform?
	you		wear a helmet?
	we		go to university?
Do	they	have to	work very hard?
Does	he		work at night?
	she		like animals?

4 **Talk Partners** **Ask and answer.**

Do nurses have to work at night?

Yes, they do.

Grammar clue

Remember to use the correct form of the verb in your answers.

Do lawyers have to go to university?
Yes, they **do**. No, they **don't**.
Does he have to wear a uniform?
Yes, he **does**. No, he **doesn't**.

Before you read

1 **Use the code to read the message from Luke.**

I wanted to be an 153–759–783–715–637–585–153–849–783 when I was young. What do you want to be when you're older?

What jobs do you think will be in the story?

2 **Listen and read. Act out.** CD3 47

Bring a relative to school day

Key learning outcomes: read, listen and understand a story about a school day

Language: *My dad is a vet. He works at the aquarium. What do you want to be when you're older?*

After you read

3 **Talk Partners** **Read and correct.**

1 Amy's mum is a hairdresser.

No. Amy's mum is a chef.

2 Ravi's dad arrives first.

3 Ravi's dad is a carpenter.

4 Ravi's dad is late because he went shopping.

5 The children go to the zoo.

4 **Values** **Read and discuss.** Whole Class

- Why is Ravi's dad late in the story?
- Are your friends sometimes late?
- How do you feel when your friends are late?
- What do you say if you're late?

1 Listen, point and say. CD4 01

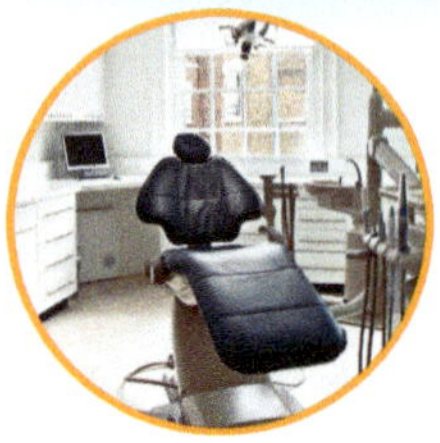
1 clinic

2 salon

3 garage

4 factory

5 workshop

6 office

2 Listen and sing *In my street*. CD4 02

A dentist is a person who
works in a clinic.
She cleans, she brushes and
she looks after your teeth.
A clinic is a place where
a dentist works.
There's a dentist in my street.

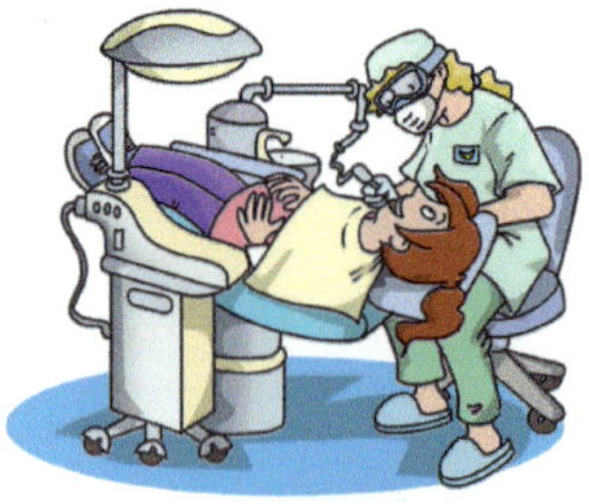

A hairdresser is a person
who works in a salon.
He washes, he cuts and he
dries your hair.
A salon is a place where
a hairdresser works.
There's a hairdresser in my street.

A mechanic is a person who
works in a garage.
He oils, he checks and he
fixes your car.
A garage is a place where
a mechanic works.
There's a mechanic in my street.

A carpenter is a person who
works in a workshop.
She saws and she builds things out
of wood.
A workshop is a place where
a carpenter works.
There's a carpenter in my street.

3 Listen and follow. Repeat. CD4 04

relative clauses

A dentist				a clinic.
A hairdresser	is a person	who	works in	a salon.
A carpenter				a workshop.
A garage			a mechanic	
A kitchen	is a place	where	a chef	works.
An office			a lawyer	

4 Talk Partners

Play a *true* or *false* game.

A dentist is a person who works in a salon.

That's false.

Grammar clue

We say who when we talk about people.
We say where when we talk about places.

Key learning outcomes: identify and say places of work; use *who* and *where* in relative clauses
Vocabulary: places of work **Grammar:** *A hairdresser is a person who works in a salon.*

1 Listen, read and say. CD4 05

Speak and spell

'er' or 'or'?

Dan the driv**er** drives and Alice the act**or** acts. Sam the sail**or** sails and Bob the bak**er** bakes.

Remember!
t**ur**tle b**ir**d

Now practise spelling on page 84 in your Activity Book.

2 Look at the picture. Listen and say *true* or *false*. CD4 06

3 **Talk Partners** Play a guessing game. Ask and answer.

Teacher's Resource Bank: Unit 8

Key learning outcomes: listen for specific information; play a communication game using relative clauses **Phonics:** Alternative vowel spellings: *er – or*

Literacy

Before you read

1 **Do you know the names of any newspapers? Do you read newspapers? Which of these features do you read?** Whole Class

news about your city   news about your country   news about other countries

sport   cartoons   weather   TV guide   crosswords

2 **Look at the headline below. What do you think the article is about?** Whole Class

3 **Read and listen to find out.** CD4 07

Reading tip!

Before you read, think about what you already know about astronauts.

Have you got what it takes to go into SPACE?

Many of us dream of going into space when we're older. But life in space isn't easy. Have you got what it takes to be an astronaut?

You must work hard at school, because you have to go to university and study Science or Maths. Many astronauts have to know how to fly a plane, too.

There's a physical exam, so you have to be fit and healthy. Astronauts have to exercise a lot when they're in space to keep their muscles strong.

You have to be friendly and good at teamwork, because astronauts live and work together in a very small space.

Astronauts have to wear a space suit when they work outside the Space Station. It can take them over an hour to put on a space suit, and they need a helper to put on all of the different parts in the right order. The suits are always made a little bit bigger, because astronauts grow taller when they're in space!

People from all over the world go to space. You have to speak English and Russian, so that you can talk to the other astronauts. You can learn Russian when you're training to be an astronaut, like Nicole Stott.

Nicole Stott was part of a team of six astronauts who lived on the International Space Station for 91 days. As part of her job, Nicole went on space walks to repair the Space Station. She also did experiments.

Nicole Stott on the Space Station

Are you still interested in becoming an astronaut? Make sure you study hard and keep fit and healthy. And one day, we will see you in space!

After you read

Go to page 85 in your Activity Book.

Key learning outcomes: read and understand a non-chronological report

Text type: **a newspaper article / an interview**

Investigate a text

1 **What questions would you like to ask an astronaut? Make a list.** Whole Class

2 **Read and listen to the interview. Can you see your questions?** CD4 08

life in space

Life in space

We wanted to find out what it's really like training to be an astronaut, and to know whether it's as exciting as it seems. We decided to interview Michelle. She's training to be an astronaut.

Why do you want to be an astronaut?

I want to be an astronaut because I love flying and learning about the solar system.

Who taught you to fly?

My father taught me to fly.

What do you have to do in your astronaut training?

We have to learn about science for our mission. We have to learn how to eat and have a shower in space. It isn't easy!

What do astronauts eat in space?

The food is good on the Space Station. There isn't much fresh food, but there's a machine that adds hot water to the food.

How much exercise do you do?

I exercise for two hours every day. I have to be very fit and healthy.

What do you wear in space?

In space, we wear our astronaut space suits. On the Space Station, we can wear our own clothes.

What languages do you speak?

I speak English and I'm learning to speak Russian.

When are you going to go into space?

I'm going to go into space next year. I'm very excited.

Thank you for talking to us, Michelle.

You're welcome.

Discuss a text

3 **Think and discuss.** Whole Class

1 Are the questions in the interview open or closed?

2 Are the questions easy to understand?

3 Are the questions general, personal or both?

4 Are the questions interesting?

Writing tip!

We use ***for*** when we're talking about a period of time.

*... who lived on the International Space Station **for** 91 days.*

*I exercise **for** two hours every day.*

Plan and write an interview on page 86 in your Activity Book.

Key learning outcomes: prepare and write a non-chronological report; use *for* to talk about a period of time

1 Read Luke's questions. What do you think?

Whole Class

1 What's a lighthouse used for?
2 How many lighthouse keepers lived on Maatsuyker Island?
3 What did the lighthouse keepers do every day?
4 What's the weather like on the island?

2 Read and listen. Answer Luke's questions.

CD4 09

lighthouse keepers

Lighthouse keepers

Lighthouses are very important for the safety of ships. They warn them to stay away from dangerous land and rocks, and they help sailors to know where they are. Each lighthouse has got its own special sequence of light flashes. It's very important that the lamps flash in the correct sequence, so that sailors know where they are.

There are lots of lighthouses all over the world, but not many have got lighthouse keepers now.

On Maatsuyker Island, near Tasmania, there were three lighthouse keepers who lived on the island with their families. They were the only people who lived on the island.

The lighthouse was built in 1891. In the past, the lamps used oil, but now they use solar power. The lighthouse has got three floors and a spiral staircase made of metal.

The lighthouse keepers checked the weather four times a day. They also cleaned the lamps. When a ship from Sweden crashed onto the rocks, the lighthouse keepers helped the six sailors get to the island safely.

The island is very remote and there aren't any houses or shops. The lighthouse keepers and their families received food every few months by boat. The bad weather made their job difficult, too. It rains most days on the island, and it's very windy. Life wasn't easy, but the lighthouse keepers always kept the lamps burning!

Think about your culture Are there any lighthouses where you live? Are there any lighthouse keepers in your country? What do they do?

Do the Tasmania web quest and the Unit Review on pages 87 and 88 in your Activity Book. ICT

Key learning outcomes: read about lighthouse keepers in Tasmania; think about and research Tasmania

21 CHANNEL

Today's programme is about jobs. What do you want to be when you grow up?

1 **Watch the video. Who needs this safety equipment?**

2 **Watch the video again. Read and say *true* or *false*. Correct the false sentences.**

1 Health and safety is not very important at work.
2 Builders have to protect their eyes.
3 Firefighters use oxygen tanks to help them breathe.
4 Doctors have to wear a helmet.
5 Scientists have to wear special boots.

3 **Look and say. What equipment do these people need to stay safe at work?**

Health and safety

It's important to stay safe when you are at work.

1
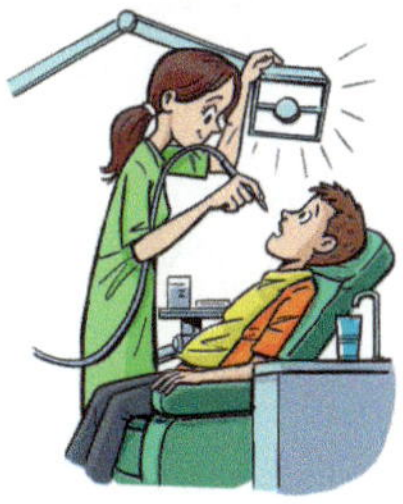
dentist

2

mechanic

3

carpenter

4

chef

Key learning outcomes: watch and understand a video about jobs
21st **Living in the world:** health and safety

Unit 9 All around the world

Lesson 1 Vocabulary

1 France

2 Italy

3 India

4 Morocco

5 Russia

6 Germany

7 China

8 Japan

9 Mexico

10 Portugal

11 Brazil

12 Romania

1 **Make a list of countries. Which are in Europe? Where do you go on holiday? Do you go to other countries?** Brainstorm

2 **Listen, point and say the vocabulary chant.** CD4 13

3 **Listen, look and sing *All around the world*.** CD4 14

All around the world,
There are different countries.
You can go by plane,
Boat or train.
You can even go by car.

There's Brazil and there's Germany.
There's France and there's Italy.
What would you like to see?
Chorus

There's Portugal and there's India.
There's Russia and there's Romania.
What would you like to see?
Chorus

There's China and there's Mexico.
There's Japan and there's Morocco.
There are so many places to see.
Chorus

4 **Talk Partners** **Play a guessing game.**

It's got a blue, white and red flag.

Is it France?

Yes, it is. Would you like to go to France?

Yes, I would.

Key learning outcomes: identify and say countries; sing a song about different countries around the world **Vocabulary:** countries

1 **Listen and read. Listen and repeat. Act out.** CD4 16

Josh: Have you ever been to another country, Grandad?

Grandad: Yes, I have. When I was young, I travelled all over the world.

Josh: Have you ever been to Italy?

Grandad: Yes, I have.

Josh: Lucky you! Have you ever been to China?

Grandad: No, I haven't, but I've been to Japan.

Josh: Great! Have you ever been to Mexico?

Grandad: Yes, I have. I went to Mexico when I finished university.

Josh: Wow! Have you ever been to Morocco?

Grandad: No, I haven't, but we're all going there for our summer holidays!

2 **Read again. Where has Josh's grandad been to?**

3 **Listen and follow. Repeat.** CD4 17

Present perfect

	you			to Italy?
Have	they	ever	been	to Morocco?
Has	he			to China?
	she			to India?

4 **Talk Partners** **Ask and answer about Josh's grandad.**

Has he ever been to Italy?

Yes, he has.

Grammar clue

We use have or has + past participle.

I've been to Japan. / He's been to France.
I haven't been to Japan. / He hasn't been to France.

Key learning outcomes: use the present perfect to talk about countries
Grammar: *Have they ever been to (Morocco)? Yes, they have. No, they haven't.*

Before you read

1 **Use the code to read the message from Luke.**

Have a great time on your holiday! I haven't been to 501–637–715–637–195–195–637, but I'd like to go.

Read the title of the story. What adventure do you think the children have in Morocco?

2 **Listen and read. Act out.** CD4 18

The Moroccan adventure

Key learning outcomes: read, listen and understand a story about a Moroccan adventure
Language: *Have you ever been to an oasis? My camel is very friendly.*

After you read

3 **Talk Partners** Ask and answer.

1 Where do the children go first?

They go to the market.

2 What do the children see at the market?

3 Where do they go on the camels?

4 What are the camels like?

5 Who's making a noise?

4 **Values** Read and discuss. *Whole Class*

- What new food do the children try in the story?
- Have you ever been to a different country?
- Did you try the food?
- Did you do something new?

1 Listen, point and say. CD4 20

1 eat sushi

2 take a photo

3 see a whale

4 play cricket

5 buy a souvenir

6 visit a monument

2 Listen and sing *Have you ever?* CD4 21

Have you ever seen a whale
Swimming in the ocean?
Have you ever eaten sushi
In a Japanese restaurant?
I haven't seen a whale
And I haven't eaten sushi.
But when I'm older, I want to do it all!

Have you ever taken a photo
At the end of the day?
Have you ever bought a souvenir
Of your holiday?
I haven't taken a photo
And I haven't bought a souvenir.
But when I'm older, I want to do it all!

Have you ever played cricket
In the summer sun?
Have you ever visited a monument
And had a lot of fun?
I haven't played cricket
And I haven't visited a monument.
But when I'm older, I want to do it all!

3 Listen and follow. Repeat. CD4 22

Present perfect

			eaten sushi?
	you		**taken a photo?**
Have	**they**	**ever**	**played cricket?**
Has	**he**		**visited a monument?**
	she		**seen a whale?**
			bought a souvenir?

4 Talk Partners Ask and answer.

Have you ever eaten sushi?

Yes, I have.

Have you ever seen a whale?

No, I haven't.

Grammar clue

We use the past participle, e.g.:

play – play**ed** visit – visit**ed**

see – **seen** buy – **bought**

Key learning outcomes: identify and say holiday activities; use the present perfect to talk about experiences **Vocabulary:** holiday activities **Grammar:** *Has he ever eaten sushi? Yes, he has.*

1 Listen, read and say. CD4 23

Speak and spell

Seven heavy, Mexican elephants bounce on a feather bed.

Now practise spelling on page 94 in your Activity Book.

2 Look at the chart. Listen and identify five differences. CD4 24

Listening tip!
Listen out for the key words that you can see in the chart.

	take a photo	see a whale	buy a souvenir	eat sushi	visit a monument	play cricket
Holly	✓	✗	✗	✓	✗	✓
Oliver and Sarah	✓	✓	✓	✓	✗	✓
Sophia	✓	✓	✗	✗	✓	✓
Katy	✗	✗	✗	✗	✓	✗
Helen and Frank	✗	✓	✓	✓	✗	✗

3 Talk Partners Ask and answer to complete the chart.

Teacher's Resource Bank: Unit 9

Key learning outcomes: listen for specific information; play a communication game using *Has she / he ever …?* **Phonics:** Alternative vowel spellings: *e – ea*

Before you read

1 Imagine you are going to travel to Italy. How will you get there? What will you see? What activities will you do? Whole Class

2 Read and listen. What can you see and do in Italy? CD4 25

Reading tip!
When you don't understand a word, read the next sentence to help you guess the meaning.

Italy

Come and have fun in Italy. From July to September, the climate is wonderful and warm.

There are beautiful beaches on the islands where you can relax or do water sports in summer. Italy is also great to visit in winter. You can go skiing in the high mountains in the north.

Have you ever seen an active volcano? There are three in the south of Italy. Be careful!

Italian food is the best in the world. Try delicious pizzas, pastas and hundreds of different flavours of ice cream. What's your favourite?

Relax in the capital city, Rome, and visit the world-famous monuments, including the Coliseum and the Roman ruins. It's a city full of history!

There are many more exciting places to see in Italy. You can take photos of the Leaning Tower of Pisa or go hiking in the Alps. You can see famous statues and paintings in Florence, like Michaelangelo's ***David***. There's fun for all of the family in Italy!

See the sights of Venice from a special boat called a gondola. Did you know that there aren't any cars in the centre of Venice? People travel by boat or on foot.

Are you ready for an adventure? Italy is the place for you!

After you read

Go to page 95 in your Activity Book.

Text type: **a travel brochure**

Investigate a text

1 **Look at the photos. What questions do you want to ask about Mexico?** Whole Class

2 **Read and listen. Does the travel brochure answer your questions?**
What do you think is the most interesting activity to do in Mexico? CD4 26

Mexico

Mexico is just south of the USA. Its fantastic climate makes it a great place to visit all year round. There's a lot to see and do. You can visit the historic monuments in Mexico City or you can relax on the beautiful beaches of Cancún. There's something for everyone in Mexico!

Ancient ruins
Explore Mexico's ancient history. Visit the ancient cities of Tulum and Chichén Itzá, and see the famous Maya monuments. Some of them are over 1500 years old.

Music
Have you ever listened to Mexican music? Come and see Mariachi bands. They're famous around the world.

Whale watching
There's lots of incredible wildlife in Mexico. Have you ever seen a whale jump out of the water? You can go on a boat trip to get closer to the magnificent whales. Don't forget your sun cream and your camera!

Food
Try guacamole, tacos and burritos. They're spicy and delicious!

What are you waiting for?
Book your holiday to Mexico today!

Discuss a text

3 **Think and discuss.** Whole Class

1 Is there a map in the travel brochure?
2 What can you see in the photos?
3 What's the climate like?
4 Is there any information about cities?
5 What activities can you do in Mexico?
6 What can you eat in Mexico?

Writing tip!

We use ***for*** when we're talking about a period of time.

Are you ready for an adventure? *What are you waiting for?*

Plan and write a travel brochure on page 96 in your Activity Book.

Key learning outcomes: prepare and write a travel brochure; use rhetorical questions

1 **Read Luke's questions. What do you think?** Whole Class

I'm in **England** now. I'll be home soon. England is famous for lots of things. Can you answer these questions?

1 What sports is England famous for?
2 What time do people have afternoon tea?
3 What are the buses in London like?
4 What is Hamleys?

2 **Read and listen. Answer Luke's questions.** CD4 27

England

What's England famous for?

England is famous for lots of different things. Most people know about the British royal family and have seen photos of Big Ben, but what else is England famous for?

Wimbledon

The most famous tennis tournament in the world takes place in London. Every year, tennis players come from all over the world to compete on the grass courts. People often eat strawberries with cream while they watch.

Rugby

Rugby is a team game. The ball is an oval shape and not round like a football. Rugby players can pick up the ball and run with it. They can also tackle each other. You have to pass the ball backwards in rugby!

Afternoon tea

Afternoon tea is not just a drink. It's a small meal. Traditionally, people have afternoon tea between four o'clock and six o'clock. They have tea or coffee, and a sandwich or a cake, too. If you have scones with cream and jam with your tea, then it's called a cream tea. It's delicious!

Double-decker buses

London's red double-decker buses are famous all over the world. Some of the buses are open top, so you can see all of the sights from the top deck.

Hamleys

Hamleys is the biggest toy shop in the world. Five million people visit it every year. It's got seven floors full of dolls, action figures, models, jigsaws, computer games and soft toys. You can even build your own teddy bear!

Think about your culture What's your country famous for? Are there any famous sports events? Are there any unusual forms of transport?

Do the England web quest and the Unit Review on pages 97 and 98 in your Activity Book. IGT

Key learning outcomes: read about culture in England; think about and research England

1 **Watch the video. What can you see in Morocco?**

2 **Watch the video again. Read and answer the questions.**

1 What material is the old walled city made of?

2 How tall is the mosque in Marrakesh?

3 Where can you eat kebabs?

4 What activity can you do in the desert?

5 Why are the goats in the tree?

3 **Look and say. Which different online sources can you use to find information for your holiday?**

Getting information from different sources

1

2

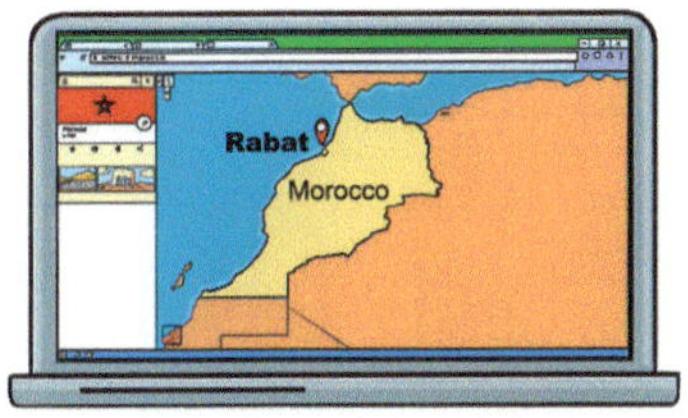

3

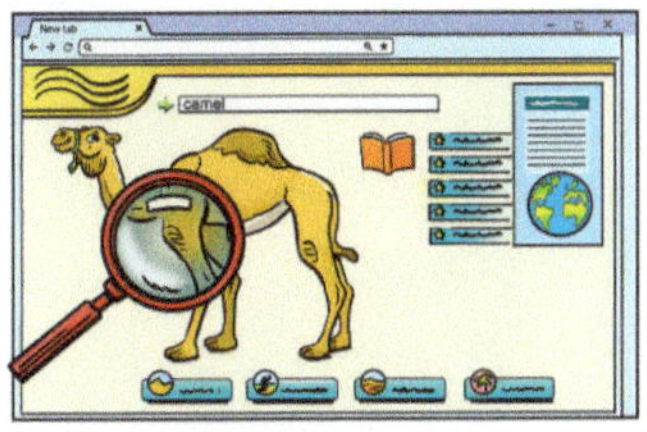

4

Key learning outcomes: watch and understand a video about Morocco

Digital skills: getting information from different sources

The medieval festival

Plan a medieval festival day.

Investigate

1 Have you ever been to a medieval festival? What did you see and do? Whole Class

2 Work in groups. Look at the map of the medieval festival and make lists.

- List some of the things that you can see and do.
- List four things that you can eat and drink.
- List four services for visitors.

3 Listen and check your lists. Listen again and repeat the words. CD4 31

Find out information

4 Find out about four activities that you can do at a medieval festival. Make notes on page 100 in your Activity Book. ICT

make a knight's shield

juggling

jousting

make a medieval castle

medieval dancing

tug-of-war

archery

face painting

make a medieval crown

stilt walking

watch a parade

make a mask

Key learning outcomes: learn the names of activities in a medieval festival; investigate a medieval festival **Language:** medieval activities

Plan and create your project

1 **Discuss the questions. Write the information on page 101 in your Activity Book.**

1 What activities are you going to have? Choose six.

Why don't we have stilt walking? We need a pair of stilts.

2 What food and drink stalls are you going to have? Choose three.

We're going to have a chicken sandwich stall. We need …

3 What are you going to sell on your medieval market stall? Choose three things.

We could sell bracelets made of beads.

Cooperative learning **Listen to and respect everyone's opinion.**

2 **Design and make a poster to advertise your medieval festival.**

Digital tip!
Use a computer to design and print out your poster.

Present your project

The medieval festival will be great fun for everyone! We're going to have stilt walking. We need a pair of stilts for this activity and an adult to help.

We're going to sell bracelets made of beads on the market stall.

We're going to have a chicken sandwich stand. We need adults to help with the cooking.

WELL DONE! GIVE ME FIVE!

Think about your project → **Go to page 101 in your Activity Book.**

Key learning outcomes: work in a group to create a poster; present the poster to the class
Language: *We need (a pair of stilts). We could (sell bracelets).*

World Water Day

1 **Listen and read.** CD4 32 Whole Class

People, plants and animals need water to live. Every day, we use water for drinking, washing, cooking and cleaning. Some places in the world don't have a lot of water. We can save water and help others. The 22nd March is World Water Day. Do you think it's important to save water?

2 **Listen and read. How can you save water?** CD4 33

I can turn off the tap when I brush my teeth.

I can use a watering can to water the plants.

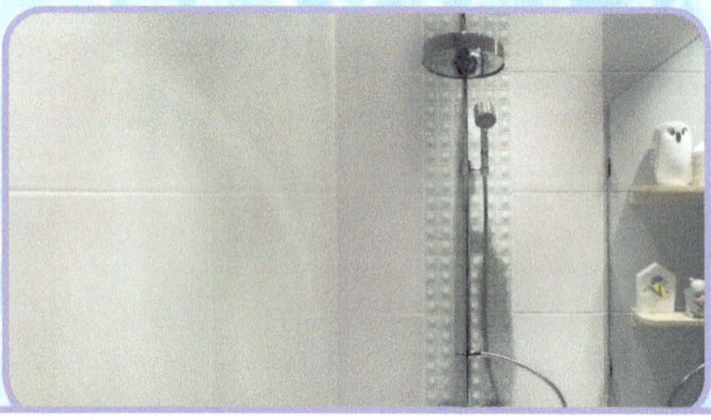

I can have a shower instead of a bath.

I can use the washing machine when it's full.

Now design a World Water Day poster.

Digital tip!
Find out more ways you can save water.

3 **Design a World Water Day poster for your class.**

1 Draw a picture for your poster.
2 Write a sentence about how you can save water.
3 Decorate and colour your poster.
4 Show the poster to the rest of the class.

ICT **Find out when the first World Water Day was.**

International Peace Day

1 **International Peace Day is celebrated every year all over the world. Different countries celebrate it on different dates. Do you celebrate International Peace Day in your school? What activities do you do?** Whole Class

2 **Make a list of words about peace.** Whole Class

3 **Listen and read the poem. Can you see any of your words?** CD4 34

Peace

Peace is important
All over the world.
Peace is for boys
And peace is for girls.

Peace is happiness,
Peace is love,
Peace is kindness
In the shape of a dove.

Peace is a smile.
Peace is a hug.
Peace is saying sorry
To someone you love.

Peace is for friends.
Peace is for family.
Peace is for everyone.
For you and for me.

4 **Make a peace display.**

1 Decorate the boy and girl in the worksheet.
2 Cut them out.
3 Display all of the children so that they are holding hands around the world.

Teacher's Resource Bank: Festivals

ICT **Find out when the first International Peace Day was.**

Vocabulary

1 Ingredients

1 flour

2 oil

3 nuts

4 biscuits

5 chocolate chips

6 sugar

7 salt

8 raisins

9 jam

10 butter

11 coconut

12 cream

2 Verbs for cooking

1 stir

2 mix

3 chop

4 heat

5 pour

6 add

Grammar

We use *a lot of*, *some* and *a few* to talk about things we can count. We use *a lot of*, *some* and *a little* to talk about things we can't count.

1 Quantifiers

I / You / We / They	need	a lot of / some / a few	nuts / biscuits
He / She	needs	a lot of / some / a little	butter / cream.

We use *need to* to talk about requirements.

2 need to

What	do	I / you / we / they	need	to	add / do?
	does	he / she			chop / stir?

Vocabulary

1 Adjectives of character

1 tidy

2 untidy

3 confident

4 shy

5 active

6 lazy

7 friendly

8 unfriendly

9 quiet

10 noisy

11 kind

12 unkind

2 Growing up

1 learn to walk

2 start nursery school

3 move house

4 get a pet

5 go on a plane

6 write a story

Grammar

We use *was* / *were* / *wasn't* / *weren't* with an adjective to talk about what people were like in the past.

1 Past simple: *be*

I / He / She	was	active / lazy / tidy.
	wasn't	
You / We / They	were	untidy.
	weren't	confident.

We use the past simple to talk about things we did when we were young.

2 Past simple: regular and irregular verbs

I / He / She	learnt to walk		I / he / she		ten months old.
	moved house	when		was	three.
You / We / They	got a pet		you / we / they	were	five.
	went on a plane				

Vocabulary

1 Prehistoric times

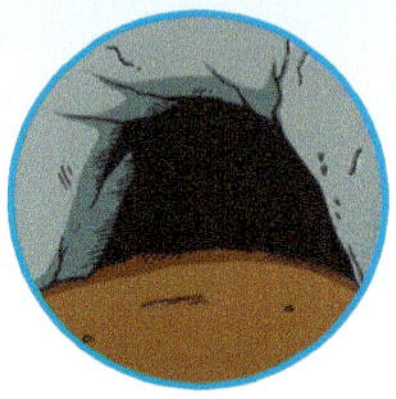
1 cave

2 basket

3 axe

4 biscuits

5 knife

6 bones

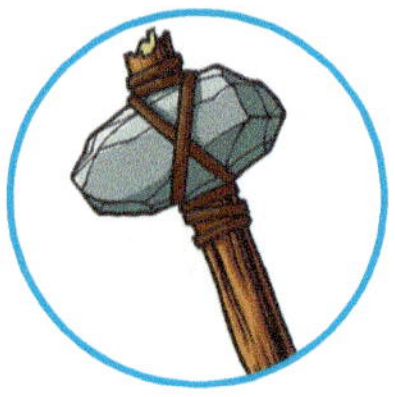
7 hammer

8 fire

9 bowl

10 tools

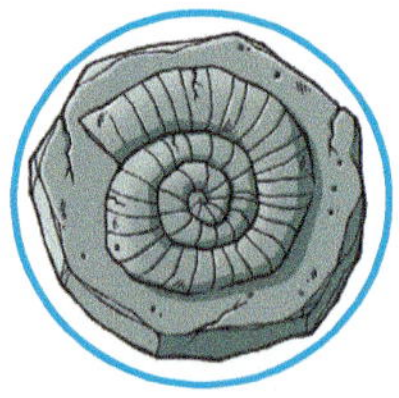
11 fossil

12 fur

2 Animals from the past

1 sabre-toothed tiger

2 giant ground sloth

3 prehistoric armadillo

4 dodo

5 sabre-toothed squirrel

6 woolly mammoth

Grammar

We use *did* to ask questions about the past.

1 Past simple: questions

What		I	
When		you	wear?
Where	did	he / she	hunt?
How		we / they	live?

We use *could / couldn't* to talk about past ability.

2 could and couldn't

I		fly.
You		swim.
He / She / It	could	jump.
We / They	couldn't	run.

Vocabulary

1 Objects in space

1 planets

2 comet

3 Mercury

4 Venus

5 Neptune

6 Jupiter

7 meteorite

8 rocket

9 astronaut

10 satellite

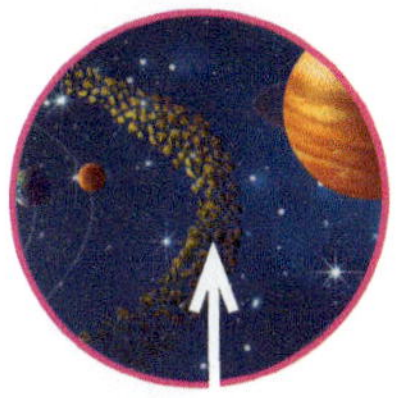
11 asteroid belt

12 rings

2 Adjectives

1 shiny

2 expensive

3 modern

4 heavy

5 powerful

6 interesting

Grammar

We use superlative adjectives to say that something is the most of a group.

1 Superlative adjectives: short adjectives

Venus		the hottest	
Jupiter	is	the biggest	planet.
Mercury		the smallest	
		the closest	planet to the Sun.
Neptune		the furthest	from the Sun.

We use *most* with long adjectives to make the superlative.

2 Superlative adjectives: long adjectives

The red rocket		the heaviest	
The purple rocket	is	the most interesting	rocket.
The green rocket		the most powerful	

Vocabulary

1 Free-time activities

1 go sailing

2 go bowling

3 have an ice lolly

4 have a picnic

5 go shopping

6 go hiking

7 make a cake

8 go windsurfing

9 play table tennis

10 go horse riding

11 ride a mountain bike

12 have a barbecue

2 Musical instruments

1 drums

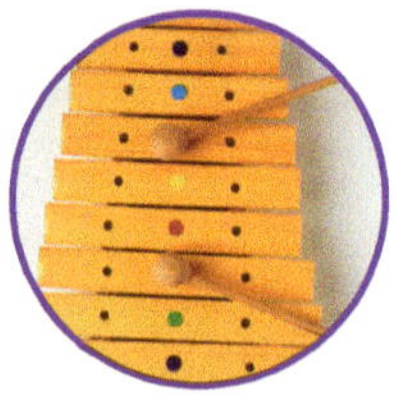
2 xylophone

3 keyboard

4 cymbals

5 tambourine

6 electric guitar

Grammar

We use the zero conditional to say that something will always happen.

1 Conditional with *can*

	raining,		**make** a cake.
If it's	wet,	we can	**have** a picnic.
	sunny,	we can't	**ride** a mountain bike.
	dry,		

We use *would rather* to talk about preferences.

2 *would rather*

		the drums / the cymbals		
I'd rather	play	the xylophone / the tambourine	than	sing.

Vocabulary

1 Machines in our houses

1 washing machine

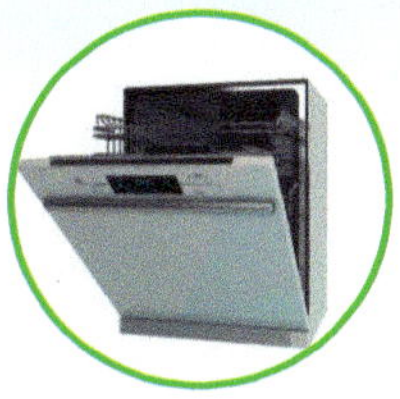
2 dishwasher

3 toaster

4 cooker

5 DVD player

6 blender

7 hairdryer

8 printer

9 microwave

10 fridge

11 tablet

12 hoover

2 Materials

1 wool

2 cotton

3 leather

4 plastic

5 gold

6 silver

Grammar

We say that something *is / are used for* doing something.

1 used for

A fridge	is	used for	keeping food cold.
A toaster			making toast.
Microwaves	are		heating food.
Hairdryers			drying your hair.

We use *made of* to talk about the materials of an object.

2 made of

A sweater	is	made of	wool.
A bracelet			gold.
Boots	are		leather.
Bottles			plastic.

Vocabulary

1 Places in a city

1 library

2 airport

3 hotel

4 university
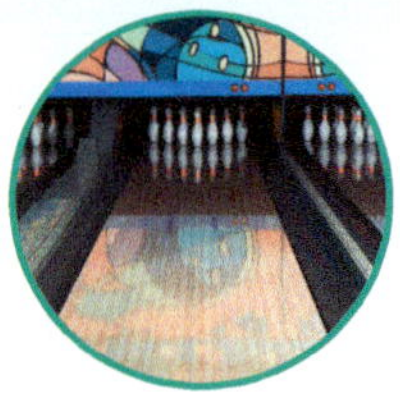
5 bowling alley

6 shopping centre

7 market

8 ice rink

9 art gallery

10 cinema

11 football stadium

12 adventure playground

2 Transport

1 submarine

2 helicopter

3 hot-air balloon

4 motorbike

5 tram

6 underground

Grammar

1 *Will there be ...?*

			libraries / hotels	
Will	there	be	ice rinks	in the future?
			art galleries	

2 Future: *will*

Cars		have wings	
Robots	will	live on the moon	in the future.
Motorbikes	won't	travel under the sea	
Submarines		fly	

Vocabulary

1 Jobs

1 chef

2 hairdresser

3 driver

4 photographer

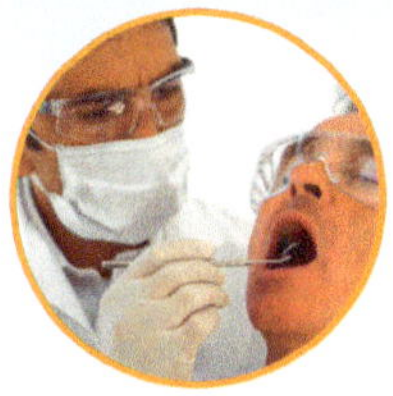
5 dentist

6 waiter

7 nurse

8 carpenter

9 mechanic

10 artist

11 lawyer

12 vet

2 Places of work

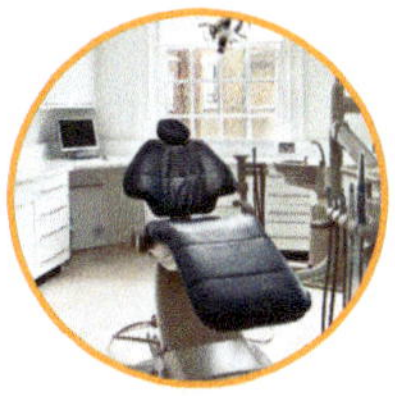
1 clinic

2 salon

3 garage

4 factory

5 workshop

6 office

Grammar

We use *have to* to ask questions about obligations.

1 have to: questions

	I / you		wear a uniform?
Do	we / they	have to	go to university?
Does	he / she		work at night?
			like animals?

We use *who* to talk about people and *where* to talk about places when we use relative clauses.

2 relative clauses

A dentist				a clinic.
A hairdresser	is a person	who	works in	a salon.
A kitchen	is a place	where	a chef	works.
An office			a lawyer	

Vocabulary

1 Countries

1 France

2 Italy

3 India

4 Morocco

5 Russia

6 Germany

7 China

8 Japan

9 Mexico

10 Portugal

11 Brazil

12 Romania

2 Holiday activities

1 eat sushi

2 take a photo

3 see a whale

4 play cricket

5 buy a souvenir

6 visit a monument

Grammar

We use the present perfect to talk about our experiences.

1 Present perfect

	you			to Italy?
Have	they	ever	been	to Morocco?
Has	he			to China?
	she			to India?

2 Present perfect

	you		eaten sushi?
Have	they	ever	played cricket?
Has	he		visited a monument?
	she		seen a whale?
			bought a souvenir?

Reading and Writing

1 Read the text and choose the best answer.

1 **Peter:** What would you like for lunch, Sally?
Sally: A I had a sandwich.
(B) I'd like salad and soup, please.
C I like pizza.

2 **Peter:** Do you like tomato and vegetable soup?
Sally: A Yes, I do.
B That's right.
C No, I haven't.

3 **Peter:** I'm going to add some onions to the soup.
Sally: A That's fine.
B No, it isn't.
C Yes, it is.

4 **Peter:** Can you pass me a bowl, please?
Sally: A Yes, please.
B No, I haven't.
C Yes, of course. Here you are.

5 **Peter:** Do you want to drink water or orange juice?
Sally: A I prefer water.
B No, we don't.
C Fine, thank you.

6 **Peter:** How much soup do you want?
Sally: A It's delicious!
B Me too.
C Just a little.

2 Listen and follow. Which picture is different in number 1? Why?

CD4 35

1

2

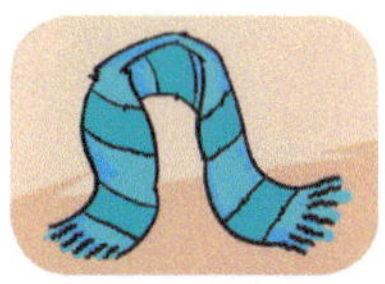

3

4

Speaking

3 Work with a partner. Which pictures are different in numbers 2, 3 and 4? Why?

Watch the External Exams Video.

Key learning outcomes: practice for A1 Movers Reading and Writing Part 2 and Speaking Part 3

Reading and Writing

1 Read the text. Choose the right words and write them in your notebook.

My friend Clare

My friend Clare **1** ___is___ very special. She wrote a story when she **2** __________ five years old and won a prize in a competition. She got **3** __________ first pet when she was three and now she's got lots **4** __________ pets. She moved house **5** __________ year and now she lives next door to **6** __________.

1	are	is	was	**4**	of	in	from
2	is	was	were	**5**	between	last	next
3	his	her	hers	**6**	me	my	mine

2 Listen and look. What's happening in picture 1? CD4 36

3 Work with a partner. Tell the story.

4 Now listen to the story. CD4 37

Speaking tip!
Think about the key words you need before you tell the story.

Speaking

Watch the External Exams Video.

Key learning outcomes: practice for A1 Movers Reading and Writing Part 4 and Speaking Part 2

Reading and Writing

1 **Look and read and write.**

Complete the sentences.

1 There are two snails on the ___table___.

2 Dad is wearing black ______________.

Answer the questions.

3 What's the parrot doing?

______________________________.

4 Where's the duck?

______________________________.

Now write two sentences about the picture.

5 ______________________________.

6 ______________________________.

2 **Listen and look. What's the difference?** CD4 38

A

B

Speaking

3 **Work with a partner. Look and find more differences.**

Speaking tip!
Think about number, colour, objects and appearance.

Watch the External Exams Video.

Reading and Writing

1 **Frank is visiting the space station today. Frank is asking questions to Oliver, one of the astronauts. What does Oliver say? Read the conversation and choose the best answer. Write a letter (A–H) for each answer. You do not need to use all the letters.**

1 **Frank:** Do you enjoy going into space?

Oliver: F

2 **Frank:** Which is the most modern rocket here?

Oliver: ____________

3 **Frank:** How many people can travel in your rocket?

Oliver: ____________

4 **Frank:** What do you have to wear?

Oliver: ____________

5 **Frank:** When did you start to work as an astronaut?

Oliver: ____________

6 **Frank:** When are you going to space again?

Oliver: ____________

A About fifteen years ago.

B Yes, we did, but it was quite difficult.

C That blue one over there.

D Shorts and T-shirts in the rocket, as it's quite warm.

E Next month. We're busy getting everything ready.

F I love it! It's amazing to see the Earth from above.

G Of course! Just don't touch the computer.

H There are seven of us in the team.

2 **Listen and follow. What's the missing information?** CD4 39

Examiner: Let's talk about transport. Which forms of transport do you use?

Pupil: I always go to school by ____________. When I go on holiday, I travel by ____________.

Examiner: Tell me about your favourite form of transport.

Pupil: My favourite form of transport is ____________.

3 **Work with a partner. Act out the dialogue. Ask more questions about transport.**

Speaking tip!

Use questions words: *When, What, Where, How, Why*

Speaking

Watch the External Exams Video.

Key learning outcomes: practice for A2 Flyers Reading and Writing Part 2 and Speaking Part 4

Reading and Writing

1 Look and read. Choose the correct words and write them in your notebook.

wood	cheese	butterfly	rocket	flour
silver	snail	dinosaurs	fridge	salt
soup	sailing	paper	cooker	telephone

1 You can eat this on a sandwich. cheese

2 You eat it in a bowl with a spoon. It's usually made of vegetables. ______

3 This animal has a shell and moves slowly. ______

4 Doors are often made of this material. ______

5 You need a boat to do this sport. ______

6 This insect has got four wings. It's brightly coloured and it can fly. ______

7 This is a type of transport that astronauts use. ______

8 You can find this in the kitchen. You use it to heat food. ______

9 This is used for keeping food cold. ______

10 These animals are extinct. You can see their bones in a museum. ______

2 Listen and look. What's the difference?

CD4 40

Speaking

3 Work with a partner. Look and find more differences.

Watch the External Exams Video.

Key learning outcomes: practice for A2 Flyers Reading and Writing Part 1 and Speaking Part 1

Reading and Writing

1 **Read the story. Choose the correct words and write them in your notebook.**

cooker	drink	4 o'clock	pepper	went
happy	bored	chocolate	smile	was

Last weekend, Sophia and her mum went shopping for a new **1** __cooker__. Sophia was feeling **2** ______ because she wanted to buy tickets for the Rocksters concert. They walked around the shopping centre until **3** ______. "I'm thirsty," said Sophia. "Can we get something to **4** ______?" Sophia and her mum went to a café and Sophia chose a **5** ______ milkshake. After that, they **6** ______ back to the shop and Sophia's mum chose a big silver cooker. "There's a surprise present with this one," said the man. "You get two free tickets to the Rocksters concert." Sophia was really happy. "Thanks mum!" she said. "We can go shopping anytime you want."

Now choose the best name for the story. Tick one box.

Sophia goes to a concert. ☐ The surprise present. ☐ The new fridge. ☐

2 **Listen and look. What's happening in picture 1?** CD4 41

Speaking

3 **Work with a partner. Tell the story.**

4 **Now listen to the story.** CD4 42

Watch the External Exams Video.

Key learning outcomes: practice for A2 Flyers Reading and Writing Part 3 and Speaking Part 3

Reading and Writing

1 Read the letter and write the missing words in your notebook.

Dear Richard,

1 I am very excited about seeing you ___next___ week. My dad and I will meet you at the airport.

2 What time does your ________ arrive?

3 After that, we will go ________ car to the

4 hotel. There are ________ things to do in Oldtown. We can visit the castle and the university.

5 It will be really great. Oldtown is ________ interesting than Everville where I lived before,

6 so I'm sure we're going to have ________ of fun.

See you soon,

Michael

2 Listen and look. CD4 43

Richard's favourite activity

activity	going to the cinema
where	North Road
time / open	7:30
who / with	friends
how / go	car

Betty's favourite activity

activity	ice skating
where	High Street
time / open	6:15
who / with	father
how / go	bus

Speaking

3 Work with a partner. Ask and answer questions.

Speaking tip!
Answer all the questions in full sentences.

Watch the External Exams Video.

Key learning outcomes: practice for A2 Flyers Reading and Writing Part 6 and Speaking Part 2

Reading and Writing

1 Read the text. Choose the right words and write them in your notebook.

1 In ___the___ future, I think there will
2 ______ robots to help us with
3 everything. They will ______ cars and fly planes. I think everyone will
4 ______ a robot at home.
5 They will help us ______ our homework and jobs around the house.
6 The robots will be made ______ metal and plastic. They will help people
7 ______ work in hospitals and shops. People will have more free time
8 ______ the robots will do all the work. In the past, things took a long time,
9 because people ______ have robots, but in the future that
10 ______ change.

1	the	a	it
2	be	have	is
3	drives	drove	drive
4	have	had	has
5	with	in	to
6	of	for	if
7	who	where	what
8	because	if	but
9	didn't	don't	can't
10	will	did	are

2 Listen and follow. What's the missing information?

CD4 44

Examiner: What do you want to be when you're older?

Pupil: I want to be ______.

Examiner: Why?

Pupil: Because ______.

Examiner: What does your mother do?

Pupil: My mother is a ______.

Examiner: Where does your father work?

Pupil: My father works in a ______.

3 Work with a partner. Ask and answer the questions.

Speaking

What do you want to be? What does your …?

Why? Where does your …?

Watch the External Exams Video.

Key learning outcomes: practice for A2 Flyers Reading and Writing Part 4 and Speaking Part 4

Reading and Writing

1 Look at the three pictures. Write about this story. Write 20 or more words.

2 Listen and look. What's the difference? CD4 45

Speaking

3 Work with a partner. Look and find more differences.

Watch the External Exams Video.

Key learning outcomes: practice for A2 Flyers Reading and Writing Part 7 and Speaking Part 1

Speaking

Key learning outcome: practice for A2 Flyers Speaking Part 1

Michael's job

What	mechanic
Where	garage
time / finish	5:30
How / go	car
What / eat	a sandwich

Holly's job

What	journalist
Where	office
time / finish	6:15
How / go	train
What / eat	pasta

Speaking

The first day of the holidays

Key learning outcome: practice for A2 Flyers Speaking Part 3

External Exams Syllabus

Unit	Cambridge Exams Practice (Pupil's Book)	Cambridge Exams Practice (Activity Book)	Trinity Exam Practice (Teacher's Resource Bank)
1	**A1 Movers Reading and Writing Part 2** Task: Reading a conversation. Choosing the correct answers. **A1 Movers Speaking Part 3** Task: Suggesting a picture which is different and explaining why.	**A1 Movers Listening Part 4** Task: Listening for specific information. **A1 Reading and Writing Part 1** Task: Matching definitions to words.	**Grade 4 and 5** Giving information about a topic. Asking and answering questions about the topic.
2	**A1 Movers Reading and Writing Part 4** Task: Reading and understanding a factual text. **A1 Movers Speaking Part 2** Task: Understanding the beginning of a story and then continuing it. Describing pictures.	**A1 Movers Listening Part 5** Task: Listening for words, colours and specific information. **A1 Movers Reading and Writing Part 3** Task: Reading for specific information. Choosing and copying missing words.	**Grade 4 and 5** Communicating information in a simple way. Expressing comparisons.
3	**A1 Movers Reading and Writing Part 6** Task: Completing sentences, responding to questions and writing sentences about a picture. **A1 Movers Speaking Part 1** Task: Describing differences between pictures.	**A1 Movers Listening Part 2** Task: Listening for names, spellings and other information. **A1 Movers Reading and Writing Part 5** Task: Reading a text with pictures and choosing missing words to fill in gaps.	**Grade 4 and 5** Communicating information in a simple way. Expressing simple comparisons.
4	**A2 Flyers Reading and Writing Part 2** Task: Reading a conversation. Choosing the correct answers. **A2 Flyers Speaking Part 4** Task: Understanding and responding to personal questions.	**A1 Movers Listening Part 5** Task: Listening for words, colours and specific information. **A1 Movers Reading and Writing Part 4** Task: Reading a text with pictures and choosing missing words to fill in gaps.	**Grade 4 and 5** Giving information about a topic. Asking and answering questions about the topic.
5	**A2 Flyers Reading and Writing Part 1** Task: Reading short definitions and matching to words. **A2 Flyers Speaking Part 1** Task: Describing differences between pictures.	**A2 Flyers Listening Part 1** Task: Listening for names and descriptions. **A2 Flyers Reading and Writing Part 6** Task: Read and understand a short text. Write words in gaps.	**Grade 4 and 5** Communicating information in a simple way. Asking and answering questions about a subject area.
6	**A2 Flyers Reading and Writing Part 3** Task: Reading a story. Choosing the correct answers. **A2 Flyers Speaking Part 3** Task: Understanding the beginning of a story and then continuing it based on a series of pictures. Describing each picture in turn.	**A2 Flyers Listening Part 2** Task: Listening for names, spellings and other information. Writing words or numbers. **A2 Flyers Reading and Writing Part 2** Task: Reading and completing a dialogue by choosing the correct response (A–H).	**Grade 4 and 5** Talking about events in the present and the past. Stating the duration of events.
7	**A2 Flyers Reading and Writing Part 6** Task: Reading and understanding a factual text. Completing gaps. **A2 Flyers Speaking Part 2** Task: Responding to questions with short answers. Forming questions to elicit information.	**A2 Flyers Reading and Writing Part 3** Task: Reading for specific information and gist. Choosing and copying missing words.	**Grade 4 and 5** Communicating information in a simple way. Expressing simple comparisons.
8	**A2 Flyers Reading and Writing Part 4** Task: Reading for specific information and gist. Copying words. **A2 Flyers Speaking Part 4** Task: Understanding and responding to personal questions.	**A2 Flyers Listening Part 3** Task: Listening for specific information (past tense). **A2 Flyers Reading and Writing Part 1** Task: Matching definitions to words.	**Grade 4 and 5** Giving information about a topic. Asking and answering questions about the topic.
9	**A2 Flyers Reading and Writing Part 7** Task: Writing a short story based on three pictures. **A2 Flyers Speaking Part 1** Task: Understanding and talking about differences between pictures.	**A2 Flyers Reading and Writing Part 5** Task: Reading a story and completing sentences by writing one, two, three or four words.	**Grade 4 and 5** Giving information about a topic. Asking and answering questions about the topic. Talking about events in the recent past.
Extra Speaking Practice	**A2 Flyers Speaking Part 1** Task: Understanding and talking about differences between pictures.	**A2 Flyers Speaking Part 2** Task: Responding to questions with short answers. Forming questions to elicit information.	**A2 Flyers Speaking Part 3** Task: Understanding the beginning of a story and then continuing it based on a series of pictures. Describing each picture in turn.

Macmillan Education Limited
4 Crinan Street
London N1 9XW

Companies and representatives throughout the world

Give Me Five! Level 4 Pupil's Book ISBN 978-1-380-01359-0
Give Me Five! Level 4 Pupil's Book with Digital Pupil's Book and Navio App ISBN 978-1-035-10886-2

This edition published 2018
First edition entitled *"High Five! English"* published 2014 by Macmillan Education Limited

Series concept design by Tom Cole
Designed by Anthony Godber
Page make-up by EMC Design Ltd
Illustrated by Fran and David Brylewska, Janette Louden, Ángeles Peinador, Norbert Sipos, Simon Walmesley, Andy Keylock, Dusan Pavlic, Matt Ward, Sam Church, Mark Ruffle, Laszlo Veres, Robin Lawrie, Richard Jones
Cover design by Bigtop Design Limited
Cover photographs by **Getty Images**/National Geographic RF/Alex Treadway; Tom Dick and Debbie Productions
Cover illustration by Ángeles Peinador
Picture research by Victoria Gaunt and Fernanda Rocha/Ikonia LLC
Songs produced and arranged by Tom Dick & Debbie Productions
Recordings produced and arranged by Footsteps and Tom Dick & Debbie Productions

Authors' acknowledgements
The authors would like to thank everyone at Macmillan who has given help and advice throughout this project. Special thanks from Jo to Carlos, Daniel and Alex for their patience and support during this process. Special thanks from Donna to José, Elisa, Teresa and Marina for their encouragement and enthusiasm.

Acknowledgements
The publishers would like to thank the following teachers for their contribution to the project:
Ana Postigo, CEIP Vicálvaro, Madrid; Beatriz García Vaquero, CEIP Mariano José de Larra, Madrid; Damián Quiralte Fresneda, CEIP Claudio Moyano, Madrid; Eamonn Healy, Colegio SEK Santa Isabel, Madrid; Elvira Robledo Gandarias, Colegio Ayalde, Loiu, Vizcaya; Francisco Javier Navarro Pineda, Colegio Tajamar, Madrid; Guiomar Yagüe Martínez, CEIP Celso Emilio Ferreiro, Móstoles, Madrid; Henar Del Gallo Muñoz, CEIP Cantos Altos, Collado Villalba, Madrid; Ignacio de la Puente Rodríguez, CEIP El Cantizal, Las Rozas, Madrid; Inmaculada Romero Fanego, CEIP Príncipes de Asturias, Pozuelo de Alarcón, Madrid; Laura Tenorio, CEIP Esperanza, Madrid; María del Rosario García Leal, CEIP Rufino Blanco, Madrid; Patricia Sanz, CEIP Félix Rodríguez de la Fuente, Coslada, Madrid; Silvia San José Paul, CEIP El Cantizal, Las Rozas, Madrid; Víctor Molinero Cuartango, CEIP Ciudad de Roma, Madrid; Virginia Escalona Monreal, CEIP La Encina, Las Rozas, Madrid; Laura Zarzuelo, Colegio Virgen de la Almudena, Collado Villalba, Madrid; Eugenio Domínguez, Colegio Virgen de la Almudena, Collado Villalba, Madrid; Silvia Díez de Rivera, Colegio Orvalle, Las Rozas, Madrid; Maite Crespo, Colegio Jesús Nazareno, Madrid; Rocío González, Colegio Jesús Nazareno, Madrid; Silvia Valderrama, CEIP Benito Pérez Galdós, Arganda del Rey, Madrid; Lilian Villafuerte, CEIP Rosa Chacel, Collado Villalba, Madrid; Cristina Baeza, CEIP Rosa Chacel, Collado Villalba, Madrid; Carlota Padovani, CEIP Vicálvaro, Madrid; Leyre Alcalde, CEIP Cortes de Cádiz, Madrid; María Andrés, Colegio Matter Inmaculata, Madrid.

The authors and publishers would like to thank the following for permission to reproduce their photographs:
Alamy Stock Photo/Alvey & Towers Picture Library pp76(4), 112(motorbike), Alamy Stock Photo/Angela Hampton Picture Library pp50(10), 110(10), Alamy/David Baker pp50(2), 110(2), Alamy Stock Photo/Aaron Bastin p17(2), Alamy Stock Photo/Simon Belcher p24(cr), Alamy Stock Photo/Blend Images pp66(mr), p99(tr), Alamy Stock Photo/Bon Appetit pp8(1, 5), 106(1, 5), Alamy Stock Photo/Vitalii Borovyk p91(5), Alamy Stock Photo/Robert Brook pp86(4), 113(factory), Alamy Stock Photo/BSIP SA p109(11), Alamy Stock Photo/leonello calvetti p34(br), Alamy Stock Photo/Canva Pty Ltd pp50(4), 110(4), Alamy Stock Photo/cbphoto p48(m), Alamy Stock Photo/victor cea p14(dish), Alamy Stock Photo/Chesh p70(bmr), Alamy Stock Photo/Matthew Clarke pp76(6), 112(underground), Alamy Stock Photo/Mark Conlin p99(mr), Alamy Stock Photo/Chris Craggs p37(5), Alamy Stock Photo/Cultura Creative (RF) pp66-67(top banner), Alamy Stock Photo/Cultura RM p66(bl), Alamy Stock Photo/Maciej Czekajewski p101(2), Alamy Stock Photo/Mikael Damkier p16(mc), Alamy Stock Photo/Design Pics Inc p21(br), Alamy Stock Photo/MARKOS DOLOPIKOS p69(3), Alamy Stock Photo/dpa picture alliance p27(3, 5), Alamy Stock Photo/Elvele Images Limited p46(mr, l), Alamy Stock Photo/Stephen Emerson p90, Alamy Stock Photo/eye35.pix pp72(6), 112(6), Alamy Stock Photo/Eye Ubiquitous p102(parade), Alamy Stock Photo/David Gee p16(bl), Alamy Stock Photo/Vladislav Gudovskiy p17(5), Alamy Stock Photo/D. Hurst pp60(8), 111(8), Alamy Stock Photo/dpa picture alliance archive p68(tl, bl, tr), Alamy Stock Photo/Food and Drink Photos p14(scoop), Alamy Stock Photo/foodfolio pp67(tcml), 99(br), Alamy Stock Photo/funkyfood London - Paul Williams p67(tcmr), Alamy Stock Photo/Gastromedia pp8(12), 106(12), Alamy Stock Photo/Jon Helgason pp60(6), 111(6), Alamy Stock Photo/Chris Hellier pp72(12), 112(12), Alamy Stock Photo/Peter Horree p102(mask - left), Alamy Stock Photo/KC Hunter p48(r), Alamy Stock Photo/imageBROKER p102(dancing), Alamy Stock Photo/InspiringMoments p81(1), Alamy Stock Photo/Brian Jackson pp24(bl), 72(3), 112(3), Alamy Stock Photo/Chris Jobs pp72(11), 73(ml), 112(11), Alamy Stock Photo/John Warburton-Lee Photography pp96(6), 97(visit a monument), 114(6), Alamy Stock Photo/John Kelly pp14-15(top banner), Alamy Stock Photo/John Kershaw p58(background), Alamy Stock Photo/Kuttig p104(tr), Alamy Stock Photo/Ian Francis stock pp8(9), 106(9), Alamy Stock Photo/imageBROKER p11(r), Alamy Stock Photo/JJ pixs pp50(9), 110(9), Alamy Stock Photo/lcrms p69(4), Alamy Stock Photo/Montgomery Martin p27(1), Alamy Stock Photo/Nila Newsom pp8(11), 9(l), 106(11), Alamy Stock Photo/Aliaksandr Mazurkevich p15(board), Alamy Stock Photo/Aliaksandr Mazurkevich p15(knife), Alamy Stock Photo/Roman Milert p64(6), 111(silver), Alamy Stock Photo/Mode Images p69(cr), Alamy Stock Photo/moodboard pp72(5), 112(5), Alamy Stock Photo/numb pp12(6), 106(6), Alamy Stock Photo/OJO Images Ltd p22(3), 107(3), Alamy Stock Photo/Open Door p24(cr), Alamy Stock Photo/Picture Partners pp72(1), 73(mr), 112(1), Alamy/Pictorium pp50(1), 110(1), Alamy Stock Photo/Piotr Pawinski pp60(4), 111(4), Alamy Stock Photo/david pearson pp72(2), 73(mcr), 112(2), Alamy Stock Photo/Miguel Pereira p17(1), Alamy Stock Photo/phloen pp8(8), 106(8), Alamy Stock Photo/Picture Partners p17(4), Alamy Stock Photo/Prisma by Dukas Presseagentur GmbH p36(background), Alamy/Andres Rodriguez pp96(2), 97(take a photo), 114(2), Alamy/sanapadh pp12(2), 106(2), Alamy Stock Photo/sciencephotos p69(1), Alamy Stock Photo/Shotshop GmbH p53(br), Alamy/sifa Image Service s.r.o. p102(stilt), Alamy Stock Photo/Anton Starikov p69(2), Alamy Stock Photo/Steve Skjold p59(ml), Alamy Stock Photo/StockbrokerXtra pp50(12), 110(12), Alamy Stock Photo/stockeurope pp88-89(top banner), Alamy Stock Photo/StockFood GmbH p16(bc), Alamy Stock Photo/StockPhotosArt - Technology pp60(5), 111(5), Alamy Stock Photo/Stocksolutions p15(pizza), Alamy Stock Photo/Stocktrek Images, Inc. p48(l), Alamy Stock Photo/Tetra Images p16(br), Alamy Stock Photo/Travel Pictures p48(background), Alamy Stock Photo/Andrew Twort pp8(4), 86(1), 106(4), 113(clinic), Alamy Stock Photo/Nick Turner p102(juggling), Alamy Stock Photo/Utah Images/NASA p109(10), Alamy Stock Photo/Valentyn Volkov pp12(5), 106(5), Alamy Stock Photo/VStock pp50(11), 110(11), Alamy Stock Photo/YAY Media AS p58(r), Alamy Stock Photo/Zoonar GmbH pp60(12), 111(12); **BananaStock**/1996-98 AccuSoft Inc., All right pp82(9), 113(9); **Brand X Pictures** pp76(3), 82(2), 112(hot-air balloon), 113(2) 98(background), 99(background); **Comstock** pp8(7), 9(ml), 15(pan), 54(5), 60(3), 106(7), 110(tambourine), 111(3); **Corbis** p98(br); **Digital Vision** p47(l); **Getty Images** pp8(2, 3), 9(m), 15(spoon), 60(7, 10), 106(2, 3), 109(9), 111(7, 10), Getty Images/Alloy/The Picture Pantry/Aysegul Deniz Sanford p16(tr), Getty Images/AWL Images/Katja Kreder pp50(8), 110(8), Getty Images/Axiom Photography Agency/Naki Kouyioumtzis p80(tr), Getty Images/Blend Images/Chris Clor p41, Getty Images/Blend Images/Spaces Images pp24-25(top banner), Getty Images/Blend Images/Dave and Les Jacobs pp82(11), 113(11), Getty Images/Blend Images/KidStock p104(tl), Getty Images/Brand X Pictures/ONOKY - Fabrice LEROUGE pp22(1), 107(1), Getty Images/Brand X Pictures/Science Photo Library - ANDRZEJ WOJCICKI p49(5), Getty Images/Nancy Brown p101(1), Getty Images/Calysta Images pp98-99(top banner), Getty Images/Vitalij Cerepok/EyeEm p49(1), Getty Images/Corbis/Fuse pp31(br), 72(9), 112(9), 102(tug-of-war), Getty Images/Corbis/Mikael Vaisanen pp82(10), 113(10), Getty Images/Creatas Video+/alisbalb p69(5), Getty Images/Creatas Video/kosinak p17(cr), Getty Images/Cultura/Raygun pp50(5), 110(5), Getty Images/DigitalVision/Image Source pp86(5), 113(5), Getty Images/Dorling Kindersley pp54(2), 110(xylophone), Getty Images/Dorling Kindersley/Will Heap p70(br), Getty Images/Digital Vision/Jetta Productions pp86(3), 113(garage), Getty Images/E+/AdShooter p91(3), Getty Images/E+/avid_creative p102(archery), Getty Images/E+/duane ellison p70(bml), Getty Images/E+/kali9 pp82(3), 113(3), Getty Images/E+/mevans pp54(6), 110(guitar), Getty Images/E+/Oktay Ortakcioglu pp86(2), 113(salon), Getty Images/E+/olgaza p95(r), Getty Images/E+/George Peters pp54(3), 110(keyboard), Getty Images/E+/stockstudioX p100(bm), Getty Images/E+/TommL p80(background), Getty Images/E+/Linda Yolanda p25(mr), Getty Images/E+/vpopovic pp115-127(top banner), Getty Images/E+/3alexd pp60(2), 111(2), Getty Images/Julian Finney p100(tl), Getty Images/Hero Images pp50(3, 7), 82(8), 110(3, 7), 113(8), Getty Images/Hulton Archive/Tony Evans/Timelapse Library Ltd. p24(mr), Getty Images/Iconica/Alistair Berg p70(bl), Getty Images/Iconica/Per Breiehagen pp22(5), 107(5), Getty Images/Images Plus/iStock/JBryson p75(br), Getty Images/Image Source pp11(4), 76(2), 106(4), 112(helicopter), Getty Images/iStock/vasosh p99(bl), Getty Images/iStockphoto/Thinkstock/Anna Badley pp72(4), 112(4), Getty Images/iStockphoto/Thinkstock/Paul Fleet p109(2), Getty Images/iStockphoto/Thinkstock/Guillermo Lobo pp60(1), 111(1), Getty Images/iStockphoto/Thinkstock/Oleksiy Mark pp60(9, 11), 111(9, 11), Getty Images/iStockphoto/Thinkstock/Elena Milevska pp64(2 background), 111(t-shirt), Getty Images/The Image Bank/Chris Walsh p49(3), Getty Images/The Image Bank/World Perspectives p49(4), Getty Images/JackF p104(br), Getty Images/Juice Images/altrendo images p58(ml), Getty Images/Lonely Planet Images/Manfred Gottschalk p80(bc), Getty Images/Lonely Planet Images/Richard I'Anson p98(mc), Getty Images/Kevin Mazur/Contributor p26(mr), Getty Images/Ethan Miller p81(2), Getty Images/Moment/Astrophotography by Terry Hancock Used with permission pp46-47(top banner), Getty Images/Moment/Fandrade p100(tr), Getty Images/Moment/Prasit photo p104(bl), Getty Images/Moment/Carol Yepes p102(face painting), Getty Images/Moment/Matteo Colombo pp96(1), 97(eat sushi), 114(1), Getty Images/Moment Open/Michele Lahey p102(mask - right), Getty Images/NASA p26(tc), Getty Images/National Geographic/Ralph Lee Hopkins pp96(43), 97(see a whale), 114(3), Getty Images/National Geographic/Pete Ryan p36(br), Getty Images/Robert Niedring pp22(2), 107(2), Getty Images/NurPhoto p27(2), Getty Images/David Rogers - RFU p100(tc), Getty Images/Oli Scarff p100(br), Getty Images/Oli Scarff p102(jousting), Getty Images/ONOKY/Fabrice LEROUGE pp64(3), 111(leather), Getty Images/Oxford Scientific/Albert Klein p49(2), Getty Images/Pauline St. Denis/Corbis/VCG pp50(6), 110(6), Getty Images/Photodisc p109(3), Getty Images/Photodisc/Anthony Bradshaw pp64(5), 111(gold), Getty Images/Photographer's Choice/ATU Images p67(tcr), Getty Images/Photographer's Choice/EschCollection pp72(8), 73(mcl), 112(8), Getty Images/Photographer's Choice RF/Jonathan Kitchen pp54(1), 110(drums), Getty Images/Clément Mahoudeau/IP3/Contributor p81(3), Getty Images/Photographer's Choice RF/Ian McKinnell pp46(r), 109(4, 5, 6), Getty Images/Photolibrary/Lisa Mckelvie pp22(6), 107(6), Getty Images/Roger Ressmeyer/Corbis/VCG p89(ml), Getty Images/TORSTEN SILZ p81(cr), Getty Images/Stockbyte p58(l), Getty Images/Stockbyte/Dan Porges pp96(5), 97(buy a souvenir), 114(5), Getty Images/StockFood p98(bl), Getty Images/StockFood Creative/Sara Danielsson pp64(4), 111(plastic), Getty Images/Stone/Thomas Barwick pp86(6), 113(6), Getty Images/Stone/LWA pp82(12), 113(12), Getty Images/Tetra Images p102(castle), Getty Images/The Image Bank/Nancy Brown p101(5), Getty Images/The Image Bank/WIN-Initiative p101(cr), Getty Images/Thinkstock/Michael Blann pp82(6), 113(6), Getty Images/TongRo Images Inc pp64(1), 111(wool), Getty Images/Tuul/robertharding pp56-57(top banner), Getty Images/Verve+/ReeldealHD Ltd. p91(cr), Getty Images/Visuals Unlimited/Ken Lucas p36(tl), Getty Images/Westend61 p59(cr), Getty Images/WireImage/Karwai Tang p27(cr); **Goodshoot** p98(mr); **Image Source** pp8(10), 16(tm), 22(4), 67(br), 100(l), 106(10), 107(4), Image Source/Allen and Kleantho pp82(7), 113(7), Image Source/Jasper White CM pp72(10), 112(10); **Macmillan Education Ltd.** p80(tc), Macmillan Education Ltd./Macmillan Australia pp8(6), 106(6), Macmillan Education Ltd./Paul Bricknell pp14(spoon), 102(crown), Macmillan Education Tld./Haddon Davies pp64(2b), 111(cotton reel), Macmillan Education Ltd./David Tolley p14(bowl); **Photoshot**/Hemis p36(cl); **REX**/Shutterstock p26(bc), REX/Shutterstock/Garo/Phanie p63(br), REX/Shutterstock/News Pictures/MCP p88(br), REX/Shutterstock/Ray Roberts/p102(make a knight's shield); **Science Photo Library**/Chris Butler p109(7), Science Photo Library/David A Hardy p47(r), Science Photo Library/Roger Harries p34(tr); **Shutterstock**/Aila Images p27(4), Shutterstock/Aleksangel p59(4), Shutterstock/Algol p81(5), Shutterstock/Andrjuss p91(2), Shutterstock/Artsplav pp12(3), 106(3), Shutterstock/Jeffrey B. Banke p37(2), Shutterstock/Gordon Bell p101(4), Shutterstock/Nataliia Budianska pp82(4), 113(4), Shutterstock/Coprid p9(r), Shutterstock/Creativa Images p91(4), Shutterstock/de2marco p59(1), Shutterstock/Andrey Eremin p59(5), Shutterstock/ESB Professional p104(top banner), Shutterstock/Flashon Studio p91(1), Shutterstock/George3973 p9(mr), Shutterstock/goodluz p67(bl), Shutterstock/Anton Gvozdikov p81(4), Shutterstock/iurii pp76(1), 112(submarine), Shutterstock/Sergiy Kuzmin p59(2), Shutterstock/leungchopan p89(tm), Shutterstock/MaraZe p17(3), Shutterstock/Nebojsa Markovic pp12(1), 106(1), Shutterstock/Marques p37(4), Shutterstock/MasterQ p101(3), Shutterstock/Jurik Peter p47(cm), Shutterstock/Photodiem p68(br), Shutterstock/PodPad p59(3), Shutterstock/Joshua Resnick p16(tr), Shutterstock/Eduardo Rivero p37(3), Shutterstock/Fedor Selivanov p37(1), Shutterstock/Withan Tor p49(cr), Shutterstock/vasara p105(top banner), Shutterstock/Tammy Venezia p13(mr), Shutterstock/Jiri Vondrous p43(br); **Stockbyte** pp82(1, 5), 113(1, 5), 109(8); **SuperStock**/Axiom Photographic/Design Paul Quayle pp76(5), 112(tram), SuperStock/Cultura Limited pp96(4), 97(play cricket), 114(4), SuperStock/Bill Gozansky/age fotostock p58(mr), SuperStock/imageBROKER pp46(ml), 109(12), SuperStock/Alvaro Leiva/age fotostock pp78-79(top banner), SuperStock/NASA p109(1), SuperStock/Stock Connection p26(bl), Superstock/Stocktrek Images p34(bl), SuperStock/Steve Vidler pp72(7), 112(7); **123RF**/Pavlo Baishev pp54(4), 110(cymbals).

Commissioned photography by Lisa Payne pp7(l, r), 11(l), 13, 14(tcr, b), 21(l), 23, 31(l), 33, 39, 43(l), 45, 53(l), 55, 63(l), 65, 71(br), 75(l), 77, 85(br, bl), 87, 95(l), 97(b), 103, 105(br), 122.
Commissioned photography by Tom dick and Debbie Productions pp49(t, b), 59(t, b), 71, 101(t, b).

Printed and bound in Brazil

2024

25